# THE MADNESS OF KING GEORGE

Alan Bennett first appeared on the stage in the revue *Beyond the Fringe*. His stage plays include *Forty Years On*, *Habeas Corpus*, *The Old Country*, *Enjoy*, *Kafka's Dick* and an adaptation of Kenneth Grahame's *The Wind in the Willows* for the Royal National Theatre. He has also written many television plays, including *An Englishman Abroad*, *A Question of Attribution*, and the series of monologues, *Talking Heads*. His autobiographical collection of prose writings, *Writing Home*, was published in 1994.

# The Madness
# of King George

## ALAN BENNETT

*faber and faber*

LONDON · BOSTON

First published in 1995
by Faber and Faber Limited
3 Queen Square London WC1N 3AU

Photoset by Parker Typesetting Service, Leicester
Printed in England by Clays Ltd, St Ives plc

© Forelake Ltd, 1995

Photographs by kind permission of Channel Four Films and Samuel Goldwyn
Company © 1994

Extracts from the author's production diary included in the Introduction were first
printed in the *London Review of Books*.

Alan Bennett is hereby identified as author of this work in accordance with
Section 77 of the Copyright, Designs and Patents Act 1988

A CIP record of this book is available from the British Library

ISBN 0-571-17616-X

2 4 6 8 10 9 7 5 3 1

# INTRODUCTION

The first draft of *The Madness of King George* (then called *The Madness of George III*) was prefaced with this note:

The Windsor Castle in which much of the action takes place is the castle before it was reconstructed in the 1820s. The 18th century wasn't all elegance and there should be a marked contrast between the state rooms, in which the King's life was largely spent, and the back parts of the building, those tiny rooms and attics, cubicles almost, where, because the court was so crowded, most of the courtiers had to lodge. This was certainly the situation at Versailles and, I imagine, at most of the courts of Europe. Greville is lucky to have a little room to himself and the pages sleep stacked in a cupboard like a scene from *Alice in Wonderland*.

It's not simply a contrast between public opulence and private squalor. I don't imagine the living quarters of the court, cramped though they were, to have been particularly squalid; I think of them as being long boarded passages lined with doors, with narrow staircases and abrupt changes of level . . . accommodation not unlike that in the colleges at Oxford and Cambridge or on the top floors of country houses. But scrubbed and white-painted as these quarters may have been, cramped they certainly were and often situated behind and adjacent to the state rooms and grand corridors where the ceremonial life of the court was led. Access to these back parts is through doors flush with the panelling or covered in camouflaging wallpaper; when Greville, say, comes on duty it's as if he's threading his way through a complicated backstage before coming out onto the set.

There should be a sense too that what happens to the King in the course of his illness is reflected in the topography of the castle. His behaviour, previously geared to the public and state rooms, gradually becomes inappropriate for such settings; when he periodically escapes into the back parts of the castle (as when he is looking for the Queen, for instance), it's comparable to his escape into the back parts of his personality, the contrast between what he seems and what he is echoed by that between the state rooms and the attics.

The notion of courts as overcrowded places I took from Nancy Mitford's *The Sun King*, with its vivid account of conditions at Versailles. Not to be at court in France was social death, and the aristocracy were prepared to put up with almost any inconvenience to avoid having to reside on their estates. In order to cope with the demand, rooms in the palace were divided and divided again, the elegant state apartments of the palace backing on to a labyrinth of poky lodgings and what were, in effect, bedsitters.

While the social set-up was different in England, the court never quite the same magnet, nevertheless here too conditions must have been pretty cheek by jowl, particularly in unreconstructed Windsor. Formality there was (too much of it, the courtiers complained), but with a crowd of well-to-do people crammed together in a tight place etiquette was always under strain and once the door closed on the King and Queen, the relief must have been as palpable as it is in the film; the royal brothers sink thankfully on to the vacated thrones and take off their shoes, and poor pregnant Lady Townsend is at last permitted to sit down. In the first version of the script I wanted to emphasize the unbuttoning that occurred once the King and Queen left the room, by having Fitzroy unexpectedly return; the court is suddenly stunned back into silence and immobility, thinking Their Majesties are about to come back; however Fitzroy is only retrieving a shawl the Queen has left, so the hubbub resumes. Revising the script, I could see that there would be no time for such underlining and it was an early cut.

'No time' is, of course, always the problem. Film is drama at its most impatient, 'What happens next?' the perpetual nag. One can never *hang about*, thinks the writer, petulantly. There's a bit more leeway on stage, depending on the kind of story one's telling, and more still on television, where the viewers are so close to the characters as not to mind whether they dawdle a bit. But with film, meandering is out of the question; it has to be brisk, so most of my atmospheric backstairs stuff never made it to the final film

– so little, in fact, that I wonder now how I could ever have thought it would, and was that preamble to the script just a sales pitch?

Not really, as the odd glimpses of life behind the scenes that did make it to the screen do pay off. There is the cupboard in the wall opened by the distraught King to reveal his three pages sleeping stacked on shelves one above the other (like the Fettiplaces on their monument in Swinbrook church in Oxfordshire). The King dashes along a vaulted corridor (Broughton Castle), bursts in upon a sleeping lady-in-waiting and demands her chamber pot. 'Do it, England,' he adjures himself, 'do it.'

But time and the budget put paid to much of the rest . . . no back corridors thronged with courtiers, still primping and titivating themselves as they hurry down to the opening concert; no shot of the same corridors silent in the small hours as one by one the doors open and sleepy courtiers stumble out *en déshabille* to listen to the distant howling of the King. The loss of such scenes was a sacrifice but they were cut with resignation and general agreement, the telling of the King's story always taking priority and so edging out some of these nice vignettes.

Besides, the screenwriter's hopes for his film must always be a little fanciful. I'd have liked (who wouldn't?) the scene (later cut) where the King, gone suddenly mad, is followed at a discreet distance by the wondering court to have had some of the suspense and trepidation of a similar scene in Eisenstein's *Ivan the Terrible*. I may even have put that daunting note in the stage directions. It can't have helped; I might as well have said, 'If it can be arranged I'd like this film to be a masterpiece.'

Earlier in life I used to revel in the break from my routine that filming provided, while feeling myself as scriptwriter to have as necessary a role as the Make-Up department or Costumes. The scene often needed tweaking, for instance, to adapt it to the chosen location; the dialogue might need tweaking too, particularly if it was a Northern piece. So I used to take my place in that ritual dance that unfolds before the shot: the production assistant calls for 'final checks' and as the camera assistant runs out his tape to determine the focus, Make-Up and Costumes dart in to powder a nose or straighten a tie, while the author (director, of course, permitting) has an earnest word with the actor about some emphasis or other.

That this hands-on authorship has loosened is partly due to age. Happy enough to sit around on the set all day if I'm acting, when I'm in attendance as scriptwriter I feel it's not a proper investment of time. Besides, many of the cast knew this piece better than I did, having played it on the stage off and on for two and a half years. So whereas once upon a time I'd have been able to give a day-by-day account of the shooting of the film, my visits during the summer of 1994 to the unit on *The Madness of King George* were quite sporadic. Here are my notes on some of them:

*8 July, Thame Park, Oxfordshire.* First day of shooting *George III*. Twenty-two years since I first went on location (to Halifax in 1972 for *A Day Out*). Then I was full of jokes and enthusiasm, watching every shot and fussing over how my precious words were spoken. Today it's raining and I'm full of aches and pains and can scarcely bother to trail along the track to the pigsty, which is the first set-up of the film – and Nicholas Hytner's first set-up ever. As always, even on a modest film like ours, the sheer size of the operation depresses: a dozen vans, two or three buses, half-a-dozen caravans, rows of cars and dozens and dozens of people, all of whom have good reason for being there except me, who started it all.

I watch the first shot, Nigel Hawthorne as George III on the brink of madness, talking to a pig, marvelling between takes at some wonderful run-down eighteenth-century barns with intricate grey-beamed roofs and sagging tiles. Nick H. seems happy enough and has at least got round the obstacle which always stopped me directing films – namely, having to say: 'Action!' My instinct would be to say: 'Er, I think if everybody's agreeable we might as well sort of start now – that is, if you're ready.' Today Mary Soan, the first assistant says the dread word, Nick simply Making Decisions about the Shot.

*28 July, Thame Park.* From the outside the house looks pleasantly dilapidated, with a handsome eighteenth-century front, behind that a Tudor house which in its turn incorporates the quite substantial remains of a medieval priory. It's a country house out of a novel and in its lost park scattered with ancient oaks an easy metaphor for England.

And maybe it still is because until ten years or so ago it was lived in by the descendants of the original owners, then was bought at the height of the Thatcherite boom by a Japanese consortium to turn into a country club. So step inside and one finds all the period features intact, a magnificent staircase, fine fireplaces, the original doors, but all so spick and span and *squared off* they might have been designed by Quinlan Terry. And (the metaphor still holding) work is at a standstill: having done a radical conversion job, the consortium ran out of money and now the house is empty, just rented out from time to time for films such as ours or as a setting for commercials.

In yesterday's morning mist, when we started shooting, it must have looked like the park and mansion in *Le Grand Meaulnes* but Ken Adam, our designer, has had a hard job taking the new look off the interior. The house is standing in for Kew Palace, where George III was briefly confined during his illness. The requirements of the script mean that it should look cold and uncared for, so the air of dereliction the Japanese so ruthlessly banished is being just as ruthlessly reintroduced, our painters still hard at work distressing the walls and pasting on peeling wallpaper. Incurious, careless, mildly destructive, the crew isn't much concerned about the house; and though Thame Park isn't Brideshead, film units nowadays are not unlike the units of a different sort that were billeted in such places fifty years ago.

*5 August, Oxford.* Most of the cast of the stage play are taking part in the film, though some of them in much smaller roles just for old times' sake. I have been given the part of a loquacious MP who happens to be addressing the Commons when news arrives that the King, whom everyone believes still to be mad, is actually outside in Palace Yard. The House rapidly empties, leaving the MP (MP 2, as he's known in the script) addressing the empty benches with only the Speaker left. Eventually the Speaker tiptoes out too.

The House of Commons has been set up in Convocation, with the adjoining Divinity School representing the Lobby. Coming on to the set, with Pitt and Co. on the front bench and the place crammed with 200 extras, I am struck, as one often was in the stage production, by how like an eighteenth-century illustration it looks.

'Do you do much extra work?' says my neighbour on the back benches. 'Not really,' I say and am thankful for it, as it's swelteringly hot and more humid inside than out because of the vapour machine pumping out steam to make the scene more photogenic and blur its edges a bit. The extras, some of them undergraduates, others local amateurs, are far more tolerant and unprotesting than their professional London counterparts. Despite the heat, they seem actually to be enjoying themselves, strolling about between takes in the Sheldonian quad, showing off their costumes and being photographed by Japanese coach parties, who maybe think that this is all a normal part of university life.

Between shots I sit around chatting with the actors, John Wood, Geoffrey Palmer, Jim Carter and Barry Stanton, whiling away the day in a fashion I still find powerfully seductive.

*6 August, Oxford.* Today is cool and grey ('Shakespeare in the park weather', someone says), which is perhaps fortunate as we have to get through eighteen or so set-ups in the day (the normal quota for a feature film some five or six). Still, everybody is greatly encouraged from having seen last night a rough assembly of what has been shot so far, the snow scenes at Thame looking particularly good, with no hint that these were filmed on the hottest day of the year. Nor had I anticipated the change-over to much more muted colours as the King's madness takes hold, Kew (Thame Park) almost in black and white, with the bearded King in his black cloak looking especially dramatic. Though at the moment we don't have enough money to finish the shooting at Thame, where we needed an extra day, just as we really need an extra half-day in Oxford.

The Unit Base is in the grounds of the Dragon School and after lunch I walk across the playing fields to look at the war memorial, a cross by the cricket pavilion on the bank of the river. Names of boys virtually cover the cross, and not listed in an impersonal fashion with surname and initials but with the boy's first name (and sometimes his nickname) written out in full, with no indication of the rank he attained or the service in which he died. After the rain there are mushrooms dotted about the field and two of the ground staff are marking out the football pitch for next season. I have a pee behind the sights-screen as the school lavatories have no locks on the doors (though at least they have doors), the bleak dressing-rooms and showers making me thankful it's not a childhood I had to go through.

*10 August, Eton.* Eton is standing in for the Palace of Westminster and the exteriors of the State Opening of Parliament at the start of the film. We film first in the cloisters, the walls of which are studded with memorial plaques to the dead of two world wars, the First War particularly. There are bronze plaques so dark as to be indecipherable, ceramic panels that look quite festive, a memorial to all the Etonians who died in the Grenadier Guards and umpteen tablets besides, some in self-conscious Latin to masters as well as boys, the conclusion of many of them, *Floreat Etona*.

A dolly mounted with a ramshackle light-screen trundles the camera round the cloisters with the actors rushing along behind as the King argues with the Prince of Wales and the courtiers scurry after them, trying to keep up. What I hope we capture is how wanting in proper ceremony the eighteenth-century mon-archy was; how slipshod and unmanaged were its public appearances, and, whatever the flummery, not much dignity about it at all.

Then we shift to School Yard, where the MPs mass on the staircase by the chapel, watching the departure of the royal party. I sit by the statue of Henry VI (a pigeon feather caught on his nose) as the coaches wheel about the yard and Janine Duvitski as Margaret Nicholson rather shyly tries to assassinate the King. Afterwards I wander down the immaculately pre-served High Street. Here is Coutts Bank and some smart tailor's, established in the eighteenth century; there's a grand photographer's that looks as if it was established not long after, and other smart and elegant shops are hangers-on and camp-followers of the school.

The message is plain: these boys are rich. And I hate it and feel the worse for hating it, because the school has been so helpful and cooperative over the film. I can see, though, that to be educated here isn't an unmixed blessing and that afterwards it could, as in Cyril Connolly's case, be downhill all the way, even the most lustrous Oxford or Cambridge college something of a comedown after all this.

I go back to the filming to find Greville on camera, knocking at a door covered, as is most Eton woodwork, in ancient graffiti. Some of it, though, is not quite so ancient (or not ancient enough for us) and it's only when we view the rushes that we see the date '1862' large and plain on this door at which he is knocking in 1788.

*3 September, Broughton.* Drive in grey drizzle to Banbury. Feel, even just passing through the town, the rootless anonymity that has swamped the place, the centre still intact and even handsome, but ringed by superstores and huge drive-in centres that service the acres of fuck-hutch estates that house its expanded population. 'Thriving' as I suppose it's called.

Broughton, a mile or two away, could not be in sharper contrast: the most beautiful of houses, medieval in a 16th- or 17th-century shell with Gothick additions, entered across a moat and through a gatehouse – almost a standard kit for an idyll. There's a formal garden, great plush borders along the old ramparts and cows and sheep grazing in the water meadows beyond and overlooking it all this rambling honey-coloured house.

Onto this rural paradise the film unit has descended like an invading army. Twenty or so vans have ploughed up one of the meadows, thirty cars are parked under the trees; there are half a dozen caravans, two marquees and the sodden ground is rapidly turning into a quagmire. Churning up the edges of the perfect lawns, company cars ferry the actors to and from the location in the house where the sparks, who have seen it all before, lug their lights and tripods down the superb vaulted corridors.

Seemingly unaffected by all this is the lady of the house, Mariette Saye . . . really Lady Saye and Sele (only nobody is quite sure whether one says Saye and Sele or just says Saye; say nothing the simplest). She's tall, cheerful and wonderfully welcoming, happy to show anybody round the house, as magical inside as out, handsome rooms lined with linenfold panelling and a splendid drawing room overlooking the moat. My wonder at the place makes me foolish and I'm sure I gush, though it's partly to offset the unimpressed one-location-very-much-like-another behaviour inseparable from film crews, who congregate at the door, having coffee and a cig and trampling on yet another bit of lawn.

As always I find I'm pretty surplus to requirements, my only contribution a muttered suggestion to Nick Hytner that Rupert Graves's ad lib 'I'm fine, I'm fine' would be more in period if he said, 'It is no matter, no matter.' I watch Nigel H. rehearse the pisspot scene, then walk round the garden with Mark Thompson before buying some plants on sale in the potting shed and coming away. Except then I call in at the church, which is full of the sound of hoovering, a friendly grey-haired man, Welsh, who may be the vicar, though I don't like to ask, seemingly vacuuming the altar. It's the bats, he explains, the church disputed territory between English Heritage, who want them expelled, and English Nature, who don't. In the meantime he hoovers.

Unnoted in my diary were locations even more spectacular. The opening concert was shot in the Double Cube room at Wilton, where the hand-bell ringers give their somnolent rendering of 'Greensleeves' ('Fascinating stuff!' says the King) in front of the sumptuous backcloth of Van Dyck's portrait of the Earl of Pembroke and his family. The Prince of Wales's lodgings were at Wilton and the Royal Naval College at Greenwich, where Wren's Painted Hall was the setting for the second concert, when the King runs amok. The long gallery in which George III sees Pitt at the start of the film and its close, and down which Pitt bows himself endlessly out, is at Syon House, as was the Prince of Wales's breakfast room. Arundel Castle doubled for Windsor. Medievalized around the same time, Arundel shares many of the features of its more familiar counterpart, though catch either of them on a wet day and they look like long-stay institutions for the criminally insane.

The title of the stage play is *The Madness of George III* and the film, *The Madness of King George*. This was a marketing decision; the

American backers somewhat shamefacedly explained that the audience might think, seeing *The Madness of George III*, that they had missed out on *The Madness of George* and *The Madness of George II*, a survey having apparently shown that there were many moviegoers who came away from Kenneth Branagh's film of *Henry V* wishing they had seen its four predecessors. Where this leaves *The Third Man* (or *The Second Mrs Tanqueray*) I'm not sure.

Many of the actors and actresses in the stage play took part in the film, though not always in the same roles. Nigel Hawthorne remained George III and Julian Wadham, Pitt and two of the King's doctors and two of his pages were the same on stage and on film. Even when this continuity wasn't possible there was often a niche in the film for actors who had been displaced: Iain Mitchell, who played Sheridan on the stage, is the pig farmer (with terrible teeth) at the start of the film. Helen Mirren played Queen Charlotte, but Selina Cadell, who had played the Queen in the second National Theatre production, became Mrs Cordwell, a patient in Dr Willis's Lincolnshire asylum who lost her wits when her sea-captain husband was drowned off the Goodwin Sands. The scene in the asylum was originally much longer, with the patients due to be played by some of our leading stage directors, including Richard Eyre, Sam Mendes and Declan Donnellan. The directors proved, of course, much more temperamental and hard to please than actors and one by one got cold feet, leaving only Stephen Daldry gamely plying a lonely sickle. Alas for his loyalty, his scene was one of the earliest cuts.

The marriage of the Prince of Wales to Mrs Maria Fitzherbert comes into the film as it didn't into the play. The Prince had married her secretly (in her own drawing room) in 1785, really in order to satisfy Mrs Fitzherbert's Catholic conscience as she refused to sleep with him otherwise. Valid in the eyes of her Church, the marriage was always invalid in legal and constitutional terms, as the Prince could not marry without his father's permission and if he married a Catholic he forfeited his right to the throne. Not that this mattered to Mrs Fitzherbert, who, sensible woman that she was, had no interest in the throne anyway. No one has a wrong word for her: sweet-natured, amiable and no great beauty, she was received at court and was on good terms with the King and

Queen, both of them seemingly in no doubt about her relation to the Prince. However, when, early in 1787, the existence of the marriage was raised in Parliament, the Prince of Wales denied it even to his friend Fox, who, believing him, stood up in the Commons and denied it too. Not surprisingly, Mrs Fitzherbert was very cross and, though she forgave the Prince, she never forgave Fox, who in turn found it hard to forgive the Prince.

All this had blown over by the time George III became ill late in 1788 and the marriage played no part in what came to be called the Regency Crisis. In my script it does, partly because the plot needed thickening and also because I wanted Mrs Fitzherbert to have her own story and not just be sitting around as the companion of the Prince. At the end of the film the Prince is seen to have rejected Mrs Fitzherbert, but in fact they lived together openly for another fourteen years, even after the Prince's marriage (legal but disastrous) to Princess Caroline of Brunswick. Rejection, when it did come in 1803, was as crude and brutal as royal behaviour often is, recalling the unfeelingness with which a later Prince of Wales, having met Mrs Simpson, briskly put aside his long-time mistress, Mrs Dudley-Ward. Sometimes it's as if royalty know about good behaviour by hearsay and can give only a faulty imitation of it, or, as Willis remarks before meeting the King, 'Deferred to, agreed with, acquiesced in. Who can flourish on such a daily diet of compliance? To be curbed, stood up to, in a word thwarted, exercises the character, elasticates the spirit, makes it more pliant. It is the want of such exercise that makes rulers rigid.' Or spoiled, as Nanny would say.

In general the Prince of Wales is more forceful and more of a villain in the film than he was on the stage or in life. There's no doubt that he was anxious to be made Regent, but he was more careful of appearances than I have made him and was more governed too by that fellow-feeling all royals have for each other. The Prince of Wales, for instance, was understandably sensitive to any suggestion, particularly in the press, that his father was mad. For a subject to remark on the King's state of mind seemed to the Prince insolent and intolerable. Or *sometimes* seemed to him insolent and intolerable. For the Prince himself to make such a suggestion (and to make jokes on the subject) was permissible and permissible too, a lot of the time, for his cronies. But suddenly they would find they had gone too far, the Prince would get on his high royal horse again and his friends would have to mind their p's and q's for a bit. It's a characteristic of royalty that one minute they are happy to masquerade as ordinary persons and the next they demand to be treated as a race apart. Like the rest of us, I suppose, they just want things both ways, but this 'Now you "Sir" me, now you don't' must make intimacy with royalty a little wearing, and friendship with them must always involve an element of Grandmother's Footsteps. Like Fitzroy, courtiers must learn to be pretty sure-footed, with little hope of ever being 'natural', the ideal somewhere between those who can't forget the royals' highness (and so are stilted) and those who forget it altogether (and so are cheeky).

These reservations apart, I found I was less sceptical about the monarchy as an institution than my colleagues on the production team, partly because (and slightly to my surprise) I was older than most of them and more set in my ways. Certainly I'm no republican and find nothing particularly extraordinary in the difficulties and embarrassments of the present Prince of Wales. It's a role, after all, which has seldom been satisfactorily filled; I suppose George V was good enough at it, but he was a dull man who was heir-apparent for a relatively short time, acceding to the position on the unexpected death of his much less suitable elder brother for whom no one had a good word, some even identifying him with Jack the Ripper. (Even the *Sun* hasn't managed to insinuate that Prince Charles is a serial killer.) But when the Prince of Wales in the film says that to be heir to the throne is not a position, it is a predicament, it's meant to be both a cry from the heart and a statement of an obvious truth.

Given my royalist inclinations, I haven't followed the goings-on over the breakup of the marriage of the Prince and Princess of Wales, or read any of the literature it has occasioned. I don't say this prissily. In my own circle of friends divorce dismays me for entirely selfish reasons: it alters the social landscape in unpredictable ways, curtailing friendships, shutting down havens and generally making life less comfortable. The Prince of Wales's marriage, I need hardly add, does not impinge in quite this way, but like everything to do with the monarchy I'd just like to be able to take it for granted as one used to do. I don't want to have to think about it. I just want it to be *there*.

However, I would like to tiptoe into a royal bedroom if only to see how far, when one party is royal and the other not, the game of Grandmother's Footsteps still goes on between the sheets. At what point is rank suspended and royalty discontinued, and is the subject, even when forgetting him/herself utterly, still obliged to remember his/her place? Toiling over that regal eminence, I can imagine Edward VII's mistresses still feeling constrained to call him 'Sir', and without their 'Sir' or 'Ma'am' royals may feel too naked altogether. Though maybe the discarding of this last rag of distinction gives them a thrill denied to the rest of us who, when we have no clothes on, have nothing left to take off. More reports please.

The parallels with today's monarchy were largely unsought, but they become more obvious as the film proceeds, the final shot of St Paul's consciously recalling the television coverage of the marriage of the Prince and Princess of Wales. (On the other hand, if one is going to film the entry into St Paul's, there is only one place from which to do it; television chose it and so did we.)

Still, the conversation as the royal family pauses at the top of the steps to acknowledge the crowds has acquired a resonance it did not quite have when the play was written three years ago.

'We must try to be more of a family,' says the King. 'There are model farms now, model villages, even model factories. Well, we must be a model family for the nation to look to.'

'But, Pa,' complains the Prince of Wales, 'I want something to *do*.'

'Follow in my footsteps,' says his unfeeling father. 'That is what you should do. Smile at the people. Wave to them. Let them see we are happy! That is why we are here.'

George III has a bad reputation in the United States, because he is thought of as the king who caused the War of Independence. Were this true (which it isn't), then he could be said to have earned America's gratitude: if without him there would have been no war, there would also have been no United States (or they would at least have been postponed). By the same token I always feel Judas deserves some sort of slap on the back, because without him Christianity would never have got off the ground.

By 1788, as Pitt says in one version of the stage play, 'America is over', meaning not merely the war but the relevance of America as a factor in English politics. In the shake-up of parliamentary allegiances brought about by the war, Pitt had sided with Fox against the King and Lord North. This so rankled with George III that he would not leave the subject alone, to the extent that when at the King's request Pitt formed a ministry in 1784 he made it a condition the King would not mention America. So when at the outset of his illness the King starts to 'harp on about America', it is a sign that the royal self-control is beginning to break down.

Fox was temperamentally drawn to the colonists, Pitt less so, but neither was in sympathy with the King's view that the colonies were an inalienable estate and part of his royal patrimony. The King's attitude has echoes today, with the monarch much more wedded to the idea of the Commonwealth than is the Prime Minister; it was one of the points of difference between the Queen and Mrs Thatcher, who probably found Her Majesty every bit as intractable on the subject as Pitt did George III. In the language of the higher Civil Service, George III was 'a bit of a loose cannon'; one never knew what he would be up to (and into) next. At the end of the eighteenth century the monarch was, of course, less circumscribed than today, and constitutional practice still permitted the crown a good deal of freedom, and it wasn't a freedom George III was prepared to share.

> KING: When people in Parliament oppose, go against my wishes,
> I still find it very vexing. Try as I can, it seems to me
> disloyalty.
> PITT: Your Majesty should not take it so personally.
> KING: Not take it personally? But I'm King. This is my
> government. How else should I take it but personally?
> PITT: The Whigs believe it is their duty to oppose you, sir.
> KING: Duty? Duty? What sort of duty is that?

It was a duty to the future, in fact, as the idea of an opposition that was legitimate and not simply bloody-minded was only just beginning to emerge. I have made Pitt say, 'The King will do as he's told.' That's a bit in the future too, as it was quite hard, until his health began to fail, to tell George III anything; he was far too conscientious and well informed for that. Certainly had he been

xviii

less dutiful, less *busy*, he would have been less trouble to the politicians and perhaps to himself, as some at least of his mental torment can be put down to the frustration of a conscientious nature. 'Cork too tight in the bottle,' says Dundas. 'The man has to break out somehow.'

Whether America played any part in causing his 'breaking out', it would be hard to say. He never wanted to be opposed and to be contradicted as ordinary mortals were was, as Willis says, one of the lessons he had to learn. Certainly after his illness he was able to swallow America as he could not before and he learned to be more sly, neatly reversing Pitt's embargo on mentioning America by making Pitt promise that he in his turn would not mention, still less propose, Catholic emancipation.

KING: As for the future, Mr Pitt, you are not to disagree with me on anything, what? My mind is not strong enough to stand it.
PITT: (*Drily*) I will do my duty, sir.

Whether or not George III was suffering from the metabolic disease porphyria remains an open question. In their book *George III and the Mad Business* (1969), Ida Macalpine and Richard Hunter argue convincingly for this retrospective diagnosis on the strength of the purple tinge the King's urine took on while he was ill. Less convincingly, they traced the supposed incidence of the disease in other royals, nipping up and down George III's family tree, attributing no end of assorted ailments to the same cause. So Mary Queen of Scots was said to have had the condition and her son James I; Queen Anne, George IV and even Frederick the Great. Although Hunter and Macalpine suggest that George IV's brother, the Duke of Kent, was similarly affected, the condition does not seem to have been passed on to his daughter, Queen Victoria, so the (rather heartless) joke of the final caption probably has no substance.

The condition presents problems that are as much metaphysical as medical. If porphyria is a metabolic disease, the symptoms of which are similar to, and which even today can be mistaken for, those of mental illness, in what sense is a sufferer from porphyria different from someone who is more routinely deranged? In what sense is all mental illness physical in origin? These are large questions and I didn't want to venture into what is both a swamp and a battlefield but felt that I needed at least to show that I was aware of the problem. Hence this exchange between Greville and Dr Willis:

> GREVILLE: Do you think His Majesty is mad? Sometimes he
> seems . . . just . . . ill.
> (*The dots indicating my opacities as much as Greville's.*)
> WILLIS: Perhaps. But he has all the symptoms of madness.
> GREVILLE: So what is the difference?
> WILLIS: I am a doctor, Mr Greville, not a philosopher.

'And this is a film,' he might have added. 'And I've not been got up in a bob wig and black silk stockings just to safeguard the intellectual credentials of the author.' So the exchange was, of course, cut.

There had to be some sort of explanation, though, if only because of the scenes involving the urine. But since it was only identified in the 1930s porphyria could not be acknowledged in the film or the play without anachronism. When the play was first put on at the Royal National Theatre, there was a penultimate scene which catapulted the pages and equerries into the twentieth century where Mrs Macalpine explained about the blue piss. This didn't entirely work and when the play was revived the following season, the scene was omitted. Trying to work out how to get across this information in the film, I sometimes wished I'd been writing for Hollywood thirty years ago, because then there would have been no problem.

> EXT. RIVER BANK DAY.
> *As* BRAUN *and* PAPANDIEK *pour the contents of their chamber-pots into the river a sudden shaft of sunlight catches* PAPANDIEK's *face and he looks up, dreamily.*
> PAPANDIEK: There will one day come a time when our master's
> disease will be recognized for what it is . . . not madness (*cue Heavenly Choir*) but *porphyria*!
> (*He raises the crystal chamber-pot to heaven and we see looking down on him the faces of Mary Queen of Scots, James I, Queen Anne, George IV and Frederick the Great. And they are all smiling!*)

Except, of course, that they wouldn't be smiling, because even though the condition is more often (though not always) diagnosed today, there is still no cure, just improved alleviation.

Monarchy is a performance and part of the King's illness consists in his growing inability to sustain that performance. When the King is on the road to recovery, Chancellor Thurlow discovers him reading *King Lear* and congratulates him on seeming more himself.

'Yes', says the King, 'I have always been myself . . . Only now I seem myself . . . I have remembered how to seem.'

The King is then rushed off to Westminster to be shown to the MPs, who, still under the impression that he is mad, are busy passing the Regency Bill. They rush out to greet him and he addresses them, haltingly at first but with increasing confidence, muttering to the pages at the finish, 'How's that, lads? Not bad, eh?' i.e. the performance has gone well; he has remembered how to seem.

Finally, as the royal family go up the steps of St Paul's for the Thanksgiving Service, at the close of the film, the King urges his family to smile and wave and pretend to be happy, because that is their job. These scenes would, I hope, have rung a bell with the late Ervin Goffmann, the American sociologist whose analysis of the presentation of self and its breakdown in the twentieth century seems just as appropriate to this deranged monarch from the eighteenth century.

The Thanksgiving Service at St Paul's did not have to be invented; it's a nice conclusion to the King's illness and needed no departure from historical truth. Beginning my career as an historian, I find it harder to take liberties with the truth than someone whose upbringing has been less factually inhibited. I have to be forced into departures from history by the exigencies of the drama, the insistence of the director and sheer desperation. Had Nicholas Hytner at the outset suggested bringing the King from Kew to Westminster to confront the MPs, I would have been outraged at this adjustment to what had actually happened. By the time I was plodding through the third draft I would have taken the King to Blackpool if I thought it would have helped.

# THE MADNESS
# OF KING GEORGE

*The Madness of King George* was produced by Stephen Evans and David Parfitt and directed by Nicholas Hytner from the screenplay by Alan Bennett. The cast was as follows:

| | |
|---|---|
| GREVILLE | Rupert Graves |
| QUEEN CHARLOTTE | Helen Mirren |
| LADY PEMBROKE | Amanda Donohoe |
| AMELIA | Charlotte Curley |
| ROYAL CHILDREN | Peter Bride-Kirk |
| | Eve Cadman |
| | Thomas Copeland |
| | Joanna Hall |
| | Cassandra Halliburton |
| | Russell Martin |
| | Natalie Palys |
| PRINCE OF WALES | Rupert Everett |
| DUKE OF YORK | Julian Rhind-Tutt |
| FOOTMEN | David Leon |
| | Martin Julier |
| GEORGE III | Nigel Hawthorne |
| FITZROY | Anthony Calf |
| PAPANDIEK | Matthew Lloyd Davies |
| FORTNUM | Adrian Scarborough |
| BRAUN | Paul Corrigan |
| THURLOW | John Wood |
| FOOTMEN | Don Hammond |
| | Nick Irons |
| SERGEANT AT ARMS | Nick Sampson |
| BLACK ROD | Jeremy Child |
| SPEAKER | Nicholas Selby |
| PITT | Julian Wadham |
| FOX | Jim Carter |
| SHERIDAN | Barry Stanton |
| DUNDAS | Struan Rodger |
| MARGARET NICHOLSON | Janine Duvitski |

| | |
|---|---|
| MRS FITZHERBERT | Caroline Harker |
| FARMER | Iain Mitchell |
| BAKER | Roger Hammond |
| WARREN | Geoffrey Palmer |
| LADY ADAM | Celestine Randall |
| PEPYS | Cyril Shaps |
| AMPUTEE | Michael Grandage |
| WILLIS | Ian Holm |
| WILLIS'S ATTENDANTS | James Peck |
| | Clive Brunt |
| | Fergus Webster |
| | Barry Gillespie |
| | Joe Maddison |
| MRS CORDWELL | Selina Cadell |
| FOOTMAN | Dermot Keaney |
| CLERGYMAN | Peter Woodthorpe |
| MEMBERS OF PARLIAMENT | Collin Johnson |
| | Roger Ashton-Griffiths |
| 1ST MP | Robert Swann |
| 2ND MP | Alan Bennett |
| | |
| *Director* | Nicholas Hytner |
| *Director of Photography* | Andrew Dunn, BSC |
| *Editor* | Tariq Anwar |
| *Production Designer* | Ken Adam |
| *Costumes* | Mark Thompson |
| *Music* | George Fenton |

INT. WESTMINSTER. A DOOR. DAY
*A hand (the sleeve military, the hand gloved) knocks tentatively on the worn wood.*

INT. WESTMINSTER. ANTEROOM. DAY
*Opening, the door discloses a royal waiting-room. Robed and crowned, but settled comfortably among her children is the* QUEEN, QUEEN CHARLOTTE. *A middle-aged plain-spoken woman (German but not in a governessy way), the* QUEEN *is attended by her Mistress of Robes, the* COUNTESS OF PEMBROKE, *tall, beautiful, alert. The* QUEEN *beckons to* AMELIA, *her daughter of four years old, and licks her handkerchief to wipe a smut off the child's face.*
*Too old for her to wipe anything off his face (except the smile) is the Queen's eldest son,* GEORGE, PRINCE OF WALES. *Now twenty-six, the* PRINCE OF WALES *is beginning to lose his looks through drink, hanging about and the usual difficulties associated with being heir to the throne, the job specification for which would have to include 'the ability to kick your heels for half a lifetime'. With the* PRINCE *is his younger brother* FREDERICK, DUKE OF YORK, *a silly boy with a startled wig but no malice in him at all. Both are in full ceremonial fig.*
*Heedless of these lustrous personages and their royalty,* PAGES *and* EQUERRIES *bustle in and out, somewhere we do not yet see robing* HIS MAJESTY. *Busy, busy, busy, except that the tentative opening of the door by an attractive* YOUNG MAN *briefly halts the proceedings.* QUEEN, PRINCES, PAGES, ROYAL RETAINERS, *all pause and take him in. Bowing, the* YOUNG MAN *comes into the room; he might be Alice walking through the Looking-Glass.*
LADY PEMBROKE: *(Whispering to the Queen)* Captain Greville,
  ma'am. His Majesty's new equerry.
  *The* QUEEN *acknowledges* GREVILLE. *The* PRINCE OF WALES
  *and the* DUKE OF YORK, *his younger brother, are standing,*
  *bored, to one side.*
PRINCE OF WALES: *(Managing to combine languor with impatience)*
  Oh, God. Come on, Pa. What's that one, Fred?
  *He points to a cross nestling among the scores of decorations*

5

*clustered on the coat of his brother.*

DUKE OF YORK: This? The other day I discovered I'm Bishop of Osnabrück. Amazing what one is really.

*The* PRINCE *is about to sneak a drink from his flask when he is spotted by his mother.*

QUEEN: George!

*He takes a defiant swig before passing it to his brother, the Queen's attention now distracted by the somewhat flustered arrival of the Lord Chancellor,* THURLOW.

THURLOW: Majesty.

QUEEN: Ah, Lord Chancellor.

THURLOW: (*Aside*) God, this place is as cold as a greyhound's nostril.

GREVILLE *is bewildered by the fret and bustle of the room. Nobody offers to help;* PAGES *brush past him and when* GREVILLE *tries to buttonhole the haughty senior equerry,* CAPTAIN FITZROY, *he ignores him too.*

GREVILLE: Captain Fitzroy? Excuse me . . . I wondered if . . . Could you show me . . .


INT. WESTMINSTER. ROBING-ROOM. DAY

*Meanwhile, behind a curtain* HIS MAJESTY *is being assembled. The Garter is fastened round a white-stockinged leg; orders are pinned to a crowded coat and at a whispered 'Crown' from page* FORTNUM, *page* BRAUN *goes in search of the box containing the supreme bauble. Baby* AMELIA *has parked her toy horse just where everyone will fall over it, which* FITZROY *would have done had he not kicked it smartly out of the way. Weeping, the King's little daughter goes in search of her papa, whose adorning is reaching its climax with the putting on of the crown. Taking the priceless and intricate thing out of its battered case,* BRAUN *spots a flaw on an otherwise flawless emerald, so spits on it and buffs it with his elbow. He is about to place the crown on the royal head when a little cough and a raised eyebrow from* FITZROY *indicate that this is not Braun's place.* FITZROY *takes the crown and does the honours himself. It is at this moment, with the crown on the King's head and his ermine train fully unfurled, that* AMELIA *peeps through the curtain, sees her papa and runs to him.*

AMELIA: Papa, papa! Papa, papa. Lift me up.

KING: Hey, hey, what's this, madam? Hey, hey?

*So, though he is crowned and in his robes of state, it is as a family man that we first see* GEORGE III, *the father of his people perhaps, the father of fifteen children certainly, the youngest of which he now picks up and, pointing out a place on his cheek, lets her kiss him. Together they regard themselves in a long pier-glass. A solid, red-faced man in his fifties, he is kindly and good-natured but nervous and abrupt. So, having put* AMELIA *down, he picks up the reins of government, the genial family man banished in favour of his testy, impatient, official self.*

Right!

INT. WESTMINSTER. CLOISTERS. DAY
*The* KING *strides briskly out of the robing-room and, collecting the* QUEEN *en route, heads the procession round the cloisters. The royal couple are preceded by an ancient sword-bearer, walking (or rather stumbling) backwards as etiquette demands, and they are followed, practically at a run, by the* PRINCE OF WALES *and the* DUKE OF YORK *and the rest the court.*
*This is not royalty in its processing as we know it today – stately, ordered, a performance as well as a progress. This is a rout, a scramble almost, and leading the scramble the* KING. *And though this isn't a Sunday run-out in the car with the parents in the front and the children at the back, what better place is there for a quarrel?*
KING: The son is so . . . unwholesome.
QUEEN: He is fatter. Always fatter.
KING: Fatter because he is not doing, what, what?
     Do you know England, sir?
PRINCE OF WALES: I think so, sir.
KING: You know Brighton, Bath – yes, but do you know its mills
     and manufactories? Do you know its farms? Because I do.
     Do you know what they call me?
PRINCE OF WALES: What do they call you, sir?
KING: Farmer George. Do you know what that is?
PRINCE OF WALES: Impertinence, sir?
KING: No, sir. Love.
QUEEN: Affection.
KING: It is admiration, sir. You ought to marry, sir. Settle down.
QUEEN: Yes, grow up.
KING: A good plain woman. That's what you want.

7

*The* QUEEN *makes the best of this.*

Then the people will love you, sir, as they love me. It is not good, this idleness. That is why you are getting fat, sir. Do not be fat, sir. Fight it! Fight it! Stop!

*The procession stumbles to a halt.*

Now. Who's got that blasted speech?

THURLOW: Here, sir.

KING: Lord Chancellor. (To QUEEN) Ready?

QUEEN: (*Wearily*) Yes.

KING: Come on. Let's get it over with.

*The procession swings round out of vision, up the stairs to the House of Lords.*

INT. WESTMINSTER. HOUSE OF COMMONS. DAY

*The House is crammed with MPs.* BLACK ROD *approaches the Speaker's chair.*

BLACK ROD: The King commands the members of this Honourable House to attend His Majesty in the House of Peers.

*The* SPEAKER *leads the MPs out of the House,* PITT, *the Prime Minister, paired with* FOX, *the leader of the opposition. A rabble of MPs follows, many of them less respectable than their successors today and certainly less formal. Some wear hats, some don't, and others look like farmers at a cattle market.*

INT. WESTMINSTER. LOBBY TO HOUSE OF COMMONS. DAY

*The MPs make their way through the Lobby towards the House of Lords.* FOX, *genial and loose-living, tries to make conversation with his opposite number, who is young, glacial and quite without humour.*

FOX: Do you enjoy all this flummery, Mr Pitt?

PITT: No, Mr Fox.

FOX: Do you enjoy *anything*, Mr Pitt?

PITT: A balance sheet, Mr Fox. I enjoy a good balance sheet.

INT. WESTMINSTER. HOUSE OF LORDS. DAY

PITT *and* FOX *lead the Commons into the Lords to hear the King's speech. Over their heads, we see the* KING *start to read the speech from the throne at the far end.*

The King in the Lords

KING: (*Reading*) Whereas we, George III, in this year of our Lord 1788, do open this Parliament, giving notice that our will and pleasure is that the following bills shall be laid before this House.

A bill for the regulation of trade with our possessions in North America.

*There is a reproving cough from the Lord Chancellor,* THURLOW, *and the* KING *pulls a face.*

Our *former* possessions in North America . . .

*The King's speech goes on in the background.*

FOX: I see that the King did not write his own speech, Mr Pitt.

PITT: The King will do as he's told, Mr Fox.

FOX: (*To* SHERIDAN) Then why not be rid of him? If a few ramshackle colonists in America can send him packing, why can't we?

EXT. WESTMINSTER. COURTYARD. DAY

GREVILLE *and a crowd of* PAGES *and* EQUERRIES *run down the steps into the yard,* GREVILLE *then marshalling the crowd to await the coming of the royal party.*

GREVILLE: Attend. Attend.

The King attacked by Margaret Nicholson

EXT. WESTMINSTER. COURTYARD. DAY
*The crowd watches as the* KING, *now divested of his ceremonial robes, goes towards his coach.* FITZROY *draws his attention to a small queue of petitioners, each waiting with a written request.*

FITZROY: The petitioners, Your Majesty.

KING: Oh, yes . . . thank you . . . thank you . . . thank you . . . thank you.

    *As her turn comes,* MARGARET NICHOLSON *suddenly draws a knife from her scroll and strikes the* KING's *chest.*

What? What?

    *There is a moment of shocked silence as he feels for the wound, then* NICHOLSON *strikes at him again, and there is turmoil.*

No, no. I am not hurt.

    GREVILLE *and* FITZROY *struggle with* NICHOLSON, *as the* QUEEN *embraces the* KING.

FITZROY: His Majesty is unharmed.

NICHOLSON: I have a property due to me from the Crown of England.

KING: The poor creature's mad. No, no, no, no. Do not hurt her, she's not hurt me.

NICHOLSON: Give me my property or the country will be

drenched in blood.

KING: Will it indeed, madam? Well, not with this. It's a fruit
knife. Wouldn't cut a cabbage. Who are you, sir?

FITZROY: This is Captain Greville, sir, the new equerry.

KING: (*Pointing at Greville's epaulette, which has become unbuttoned
in the struggle*) Well, you're undressed, sir, do yourself up,
sir. You're an equerry, not a scarecrow.
*GREVILLE retires to adjust his dress.*

NICHOLSON: I have a property due to me from the Crown of
England.
*NICHOLSON is hustled away.*

QUEEN: You murderous fiend! (*Embracing KING*) Oh, thank God
I have you yet.

KING: Do not fuss, madam. The King has no wound, just a torn
waistcoat.

PRINCE OF WALES: (*Aside to the DUKE OF YORK*) One would
consider that almost as vexing.

KING: What was that?

PRINCE OF WALES: I was rejoicing, sir, that you are unharmed.
*They are now getting into their coaches.*

QUEEN: (*Bitterly*) The son rejoices. The Prince of Wales rejoices.
Faugh!

DUKE OF YORK: Me too, Pa. God save the King and so on.
*The QUEEN gets into the coach as PITT and THURLOW come
hurrying down the steps and over to the KING, who is now on the
steps of the coach.*

PITT: Your Majesty.

KING: Ah ha, Mr Pitt. Well you've had a lucky escape, what,
what?

PITT: I, Your Majesty?

KING: Yes, you. You're my Prime Minister. I chose you. If
anything happens to me, you'll be out, what, what, and Mr
Fox will be in, hey, hey.

PITT: I think there's no danger of that, sir.

KING: Right! Back to Windsor.
*As the coaches move off, the QUEEN calls to the PRINCE OF
WALES, who is in his own coach.*

QUEEN: George, smile, you lazy hound. It's what you're paid for.
Smile and wave. Come on, everybody, smile and wave.

Everybody smile and wave, smile and wave.

*The* PRINCE OF WALES *sinks back out of view, leaving only his languid hand acknowledging the cheers of the crowd.*

INT. WESTMINSTER. ROBING-ROOM. DAY

*The* KING *gone, all ceremony is abandoned, the* PAGES *bundle up the royal robes, toss the crown between them before they put it back in its box and hurry to depart.*

INT. COACH. DAY

GREVILLE *crammed into the coach with all the* PAGES, *innumerable boxes, etc.* en route *for Windsor.*

EXT. WINDSOR. DUSK

*Establishing shot of Windsor with the King's coach entering the castle as servants run across the green to attend the royal party as they disembark.*

INT. CARLTON HOUSE. PRINCE OF WALES'S BEDROOM.
NIGHT

*The* PRINCE OF WALES *is in bed, waiting for* MARIA
FITZHERBERT, *who is at her prayers.* MARIA *is warm, pretty and not very clever. She is genuinely devoted to the* PRINCE *and tries to believe the best of him.*

PRINCE OF WALES: Pa's right. I am getting fatter.

MARIA: I don't mind that.

PRINCE OF WALES: What do you mind?

MARIA: That the world thinks I am just your mistress, that's what I mind.

PRINCE OF WALES: You shall be Queen one day, the whole bag of tricks, I am determined.

MARIA: (*Shaking her head*) I just don't want to be thought a Catholic whore.

*She gets into bed.*

George.

PRINCE OF WALES: Mmmm?

MARIA: If you tried harder to get on with the King, you could tell him the truth and . . .

PRINCE OF WALES: He'd forgive me?

*He laughs, kissing her.*
You are a sweet, silly creature.
MARIA: Try, George.
*The* PRINCE OF WALES *looks fed up.*

EXT. WINDSOR GREAT PARK. DAY
*An avenue of trees, with Windsor Castle in the background. It is early
morning. The* KING *is riding hard and* FITZROY *is finding it difficult
to keep up.*

EXT. WINDSOR PARK. DAY
*Close-ups of the* KING's *hot and sweating face.*

EXT. COUNTRYSIDE NEAR A FARM. DAY
*The* KING *reins his horse in and we hear the sound of screaming. The*
KING *turns his horse, sniffing the air.*
KING: Pigs! Come on, boy, come on.

EXT. FARMYARD. DAY
*The* KING *rides into a yard with some pigsties and dismounts.*
KING: I say, these are fine specimens. What are they, Tamworths,
    what?
FARMER: If it please Your Majesty.
KING: Yes, oh yes. Fine breed. Plenty of meat on them, hey? Big
    litter. Show me the youngster, what, what? Yes, that's the
    one. Yes, I say, hey hey. You know what you are, don't you?
    You're a Tamworth. Really? Are you really?
    *Beaming, the* KING *holds the squealing piglet up to his face and
    talks to it.* FITZROY *looks on with some disapproval.*
    *Cut from the pandemonium of the farmyard to the sudden quiet
    of . . .*

INT. WINDSOR. THE LIBRARY. DAY
*At the far end of a long library the* KING *is signing warrants and state
papers handed to him by* PITT, *who stands stiffly by.*
*The* KING *takes care to look through each paper before signing it.*
KING: Married yet, Mr Pitt, what, what?
PITT: No, sir.
KING: Got your eye on anybody then, hey?

13

The King, a pig and a farmer

PITT: No, sir.

KING: A man should marry. Yes, yes. Best thing I ever did. And children, you see. Children. Great comfort, of course.

*He looks at one of the warrants he is signing.*

This fellow we're putting in as professor at Oxford, was his father Canon of Westminster?

PITT: I've no idea, sir.

KING: Yes, yes. Phillips. That's the father. This is the son. And the daughter married the organist at Norwich Cathedral. Sharpe. Yes, and their son is the painter. And the other son is a master at Eton. And he married somebody's niece.

*He tries to think whom.*

PITT: Your Majesty's knowledge of even the lowest of your appointments never ceases to astonish me.

KING: What's happened to Mr Fox?

PITT *simply raises his eyebrows.*

Such a dodger. Reform! And too many ideas. Not like you, Mr Pitt. You don't have ideas. Well, you have one very big idea: balancing the books. And a very good idea it is to have too, what, what? The best. And one with which I absolutely agree, as I agree with you, Mr Pitt, on everything, apart from the place we must not mention.

*The KING goes over to a globe and runs his finger along the coastline of North America. PITT says nothing.*

The colonies.

PITT: They're now called the United States, sir.

KING: Are they? Goodness me! The United States. Well, I haven't mentioned them. I prefer not to, whatever they're called.

*PITT, unable to restrain himself, speaks again.*

PITT: They are a fact, sir.

*The KING turns, furious, and thrusts his face into PITT's and seems about to explode, then suddenly the thunder evaporates.*

KING: The vicar of Lichfield.

PITT: Sir?

KING: The vicar of Lichfield. It was his niece that married the second son of the organist at Norwich Cathedral. Good-night, Mr Pitt.

PITT: Good-night, Your Majesty.

George III and Queen Charlotte

The KING *returns to his desk, as* PITT *gathers up his papers, bows and walks backwards the whole length of the enormous library.*

INT. WINDSOR. DRAWING-ROOM. NIGHT
*A line of hand-bell players perform an exquisitely boring (and* slow*) version of 'Greensleeves' for the benefit of the* KING *and* QUEEN *and the court. The* KING *and* QUEEN *listening with rapt attention and seem actually to be enjoying themselves. But then they are sitting down; everybody else, the* PRINCE OF WALES *and the* DUKE OF YORK *included, is standing and wilting with boredom and fatigue.*
*As they pretend to listen, the* COURT LADIES *are sizing up the charms of the new equerry,* GREVILLE, *and whispering behind their fans.*
GREVILLE, *a shy young man, is uncomfortably aware of their attentions. We note that one of the ladies is heavily pregnant visibly distressed.*
*Eventually the bell-ringers reach their somnolent conclusion and the* KING *bursts into applause, in which he is joined by the* QUEEN *and (less enthusiastically) by the court.*
KING: (*Turning round and getting the* COURTIERS *to clap louder*)
    Fascinating stuff, what, what? Let's have it again.
    *The hand-bells start again. The court dies of boredom.*

16

INT. WINDSOR. DRAWING-ROOM. NIGHT
*The pregnant* LADY-IN-WAITING *whispers to* LADY PEMBROKE.
LADY PEMBROKE *waits until the* QUEEN *acknowledges her, then murmurs something in her ear.*
LADY PEMBROKE: Your Majesty, Lady Townsend wishes to sit down.
QUEEN: Certainly not.
KING: What?
QUEEN: Lady Townsend. Wants to sit down.
KING: What for?
> *The* QUEEN *whispers to him.*
> So? You've had *fifteen* children. (*Raising his voice so that the court can hear.*) If everybody who is having a baby wants to sit, the next thing it will be everybody with gout. Before long the place will look like a Turkish harem, what, what? Oh, that's enough.
> *He stops the music.*
> Thank you, gentlemen, thank you.
> The KING *strides out in a huff, with the* QUEEN *hurrying after him, followed by* LADY PEMBROKE, FITZROY *and* GREVILLE. *As the doors close on them, the* COURTIERS *sink exhausted into chairs, with the* PRINCE OF WALES *and the* DUKE OF YORK *flinging themselves on to the newly vacated thrones, kicking off their shoes and groaning with relief.*

INT. WINDSOR. KING'S APARTMENTS. DRESSING-ROOM. NIGHT
KING (*Patting* GREVILLE'S *shoulder at the newly fastened epaulette*) Ah, Greville. Good. Thank you. Oh, yes, that's better, what, what?
GREVILLE: (*Looking at the* KING *and smiling*) Your Majesty.
KING: Yes. You don't look at the King, Greville. Didn't they tell you that?
GREVILLE: Forgot, sir.
KING: Well, don't forget.
> LADY PEMBROKE *appears, carrying a candlestick, indicating that the* QUEEN *is ready to retire.*
> Now, that's Lady Pembroke. Handsome woman, what? Daughter of the Duke of Marlborough. Stuff of generals.

17

Blood of Blenheim. Husband an utter rascal. Eloped in a packet-boat.

*A look passes between* GREVILLE *and* LADY PEMBROKE, *as the* KING *goes into the Queen's bedroom.*

INT. WINDSOR. KING'S APARTMENTS. QUEEN'S BEDROOM. NIGHT

*The* QUEEN *is sitting up in bed in her nightcap, tatting.*

KING: Good-evening, Mrs King.

QUEEN: Good-evening, Mr King.

KING: When we get this far I call it dandy, hey?

QUEEN: Yes, Mr King.

*The* KING *is restless and uncomfortable. He takes the* QUEEN's *hand and puts it on his belly.*

KING: I ate a pear at supper.

QUEEN: Two pears, sir. It is as tight as a drum.

*She gives him an affectionate hug.*

KING: Saving your presence, I will try a fart.

*He does so unsuccessfully.*

QUEEN: No?

*He shakes his head.*

KING: Cold fish, Pitt. Never smiles.

QUEEN: He works hard, though.

KING: Never stops. Drinks, they say.

QUEEN: They all drink.

KING: His father, poor man, went mad. Doesn't show any sign of that. Well, not at the moment anyway.

*They both laugh, but then* KING *cries out in pain.*

Pain in my belly now.

QUEEN: Oh, George!

*He begins to groan and shout.*

KING: Oh, oh!

QUEEN: Help! Help us! Help!

INT. WINDSOR. KING'S APARTMENTS. DRAWING-ROOM. DAY

*Peering through the keyhole into the King's bedroom is the portly figure of the King's First Physician,* SIR GEORGE BAKER.

BAKER: He looks well enough. I sent over some senna. Was that given to him?

GREVILLE: Yes. The pain got worse.

BAKER: Whereabouts was the pain?

GREVILLE: Would it not be better to ask His Majesty that?

BAKER: How long have you been in waiting? I cannot address His Majesty until he addresses me. I cannot enquire after His Majesty's symptoms until he chooses to inform me of them.

GREVILLE: Sir George. Whatever his situation His Majesty is but a man . . .

BAKER: You're the King's equerry with radical notions like that? Good God. With any patient I undertake a physical examination only as a last resort; it is an intolerable intrusion on a gentleman's privacy. With His Majesty it is unthinkable.

*Shouts of 'Sharp! Sharp! The King! The King!' The* KING *comes in, followed by the* PAGES.

KING: Ah, Baker. Yes, a ninny, what, what? Well, you can tell him I am much better. I had a pretty smart bilious attack, very smart indeed, but it has passed.

BAKER: Sir. Would it be possible to take His Majesty's pulse?

GREVILLE: Would it be possible to take Your Majesty's pulse, sir?

KING: Yes, go on. Do it. Do it, do it. Do not faff, sir. Hold it, do not fondle it. Now, were you responsible for the senna, Baker, what, what?

BAKER: I prescribed it for Your Majesty, yes, sir.

KING: Then you are a fool, Baker, what, what?

BAKER: It's only a mild purgative, sir.

KING: Mild, sir, mild? Fourteen motions and you call it mild! I could have manured the whole parish. Well, if two glasses of it can lay the King low, it could be the end of all government.

BAKER: Two glasses? Your Majesty was only supposed to take three spoonfuls.

KING: When did three spoonsful of anything do anybody any good? Measure the medicine to the man, Baker. How is the pulse?

BAKER: It's very fast, sir.

KING: Good, good.

BAKER: Your Majesty would probably feel better after a warm bath. A warm bath has a most settling effect on the spirits.

KING: Yes, well, you have one, then. Your spirits are more agitated than mine. Come on.

*The* KING *rushes out of the room.* FITZROY *looks at* GREVILLE *as if he ought to know what is expected of him.* GREVILLE *hesitates, then rushes after the* KING, *together with* PAPANDIEK, *the nicest of the King's* PAGES.

EXT. WINDSOR GREAT PARK. DAY

*The* KING *walks very briskly along, talking so fast it is almost nonsense.* GREVILLE *and* PAPANDIEK *are finding it hard to keep up.*

KING: Breathe this air, Mr Greville. Breathe it. Come on, lads, keep up. Keep up.

*He slashes at thistles.*

This is the way we deal with America, sir. I'll teach you, sirs. Take that, Mr Colonist! And that sir! And that!

GREVILLE: Fetch the Queen.

PAPANDIEK *runs back.*

EXT. ANOTHER PART OF WINDSOR GREAT PARK. DAY

*A cricket match is in progress in the park. The* KING *interrupts it, marching straight to the wicket.*

KING: No, no, no, no, that's not cricket, you don't hold the bat like that, man.

*The* KING *seizes the bat from a startled* BOY *and clouts the ball for six. There is general acclamation from the other* PLAYERS *and the* KING *is delighted.*

*Now the* QUEEN *and* LADY PEMBROKE, *followed by* FITZROY *and the* PAGES, *come hurrying across the park.*

QUEEN: What is he doing?

*Bored with being a batsman, the* KING *is now fielding; the monarch, after all, is expected to be an all-rounder. He stumps the young* BATSMAN, *whipping off the bails, and the* UMPIRE, *more out of deference than fair play, gives the* BATSMAN *out. The* KING *then throws the ball in the air and is again congratulated by the sycophantic young cricketers.*

*The* QUEEN *puts a good face on this, smiling bravely and even applauding as if this were the* KING's *normal behaviour.* FITZROY *applauds more politely, but he is not deceived.*

The King on the verge of madness

KING: Over there, out of the way, ha. How's that?
FITZROY: Oh, God.

INT. WESTMINSTER. HOUSE OF COMMONS. LOBBY. DAY
*With MPs passing to and fro,* PITT, *his colleague* DUNDAS, *Lord
Chancellor* THURLOW *and* FITZROY *confer in a corner of the Lobby.*
FITZROY: The following day he rose before dawn, went down to
　　the Provost of Eton's lodgings and by persistent battering on
　　the door roused the Provost and commanded him to show
　　him the chapel.
THURLOW: So?
FITZROY: Well, Lord Chancellor, it was still dark.
PITT: Have we come to the end of this catalogue of regal
　　noncomformities? Because I have heard nothing to suggest
　　his Majesty's behaviour is in any way unusual.
FITZROY: (*Knowing this is a trump card*) He also harps on
　　America. The colonies.
　　*At this* PITT *turns and looks, and there is a slight pause.* PITT
　　*nods to* DUNDAS. DUNDAS *steers* FITZROY *away.*
DUNDAS: Captain Fitzroy. For the strongest reasons, both foreign
　　and domestic, a degree of discretion. And a hold on public
　　functions. No levees or concerts. Just . . . just . . .
　　*He indicates that things should be damped down.* FITZROY *nods
　　imperceptibly.*
THURLOW: The cork's too tight in the bottle, that's the trouble.
　　He must be the first King of England not to have a mistress.
PITT: Fifteen children seem to me to indicate a degree of
　　conscientiousness in that regard.
THURLOW: I'm talking of pleasure, not duty. Actually, there was
　　a mysterious illness once before, in your father's time;
　　government was at a standstill.
DUNDAS: (*Returning*) Well, it was of no consequence.
THURLOW: It was of no consequence because he recovered.
PITT: It was of no consequence because the Prince of Wales was
　　then a child of three. It was of no consequence because Mr
　　Fox and his friends were not perched in the rafters waiting to
　　come in. We consider ourselves blessed in our constitution.
　　We tell ourselves our Parliament is the envy of the world.
　　But we live in the health and well-being of the Sovereign as

22

much as any vizier does the Sultan.

THURLOW: And the Sultan orders it better. He has his son and heir strangled.


EXT. CARLTON HOUSE. DAY
FITZROY *hurrying through the courtyard.*


INT. CARLTON HOUSE. DINING-ROOM. DAY
FITZROY *has finished reporting to the* PRINCE OF WALES, DUKE OF YORK *and* DR RICHARD WARREN, *the Prince's personal physician. The sound of company next door.*
PRINCE OF WALES: Cricket? Pa?
DUKE OF YORK: Howzat, what, what?
PRINCE OF WALES: Well played, hey, hey?
*Laughter.*
FITZROY: To watch, sir, it was quite distasteful. He was not himself.
PRINCE OF WALES: Warren, what do you think?
WARREN: I am not the King's doctor.
PRINCE OF WALES: No, nor ever will be. He's more likely to go to my tailor than my doctor.
FITZROY: But, sir, this is not the same.
PRINCE OF WALES: Could he be ill?
WARREN: (*Pausing, before bringing in the diagnosis the* PRINCE *plainly wants*) Ye-es.
*They go into the breakfast room.*


INT. CARLTON HOUSE. BREAKFAST-ROOM. DAY
ALL: Good-morning, sir.
PRINCE OF WALES: Sherry, what would happen if the King were ill? I mean gravely ill.
SHERIDAN: Your Royal Highness would have to be declared Regent.
DUKE OF YORK: Regent?
SHERIDAN: King in all but name.
PRINCE OF WALES: With all the powers?
FOX: Subject to Parliament.
PRINCE OF WALES: Charles, don't quibble.
FOX: And certainly all the funds.

PRINCE OF WALES: Just think of it. Regent.
> *Indicating* FOX.
> Prime Minister!
FOX: America forgiven.
PRINCE OF WALES: London rebuilt.
FOX: Parliament reformed.
PRINCE OF WALES: A palace on Primrose Hill!
FOX: The slave trade abolished.
PRINCE OF WALES: (*Tetchily*) Oh, yes, all that too.
FOX: Sir. Is he ill?
PRINCE OF WALES: (*Lamely*) He's not well.
> *General laughter.*
> I know, I know. One day. One day.

INT. WINDSOR. KING'S APARTMENTS. KING'S BEDROOM.
DAWN
*The KING lies awake, the QUEEN sleeping beside him. Troubled, he gets up and wanders into his dressing-room.*
KING: It's four o'clock. Where are you, sirs? What's this? The King is unattended. Up with you, sirs. Braun! Fortnum! Papandiek!
> *Though he is hurrying and bustling about, as he continues to do throughout the scene, the KING now has some difficulty with his legs.*
> Where are you, sirs?

INT. WINDSOR. PAGES' CUPBOARD. DAWN
*The KING flings open the door of what seems like a cupboard in the wall of his bedroom and we see three or four bunks inside, the PAGES stacked in them. They begin to tumble out.*
PAPANDIEK: What's the matter, sir?
KING: The matter is, sir, that it is morning. That is the matter. Morning is the matter. Not being attended to is the matter.
PAPANDIEK: What is it, sir?
KING: And don't mutter. Or mutter will be the matter.
PAPANDIEK: (*Trying to dress as he follows the KING*) What time is it, sir?
> *The KING hurries through to the dressing-room.*

INT. WINDSOR. KING'S APARTMENTS. DRESSING-ROOM.
DAWN

KING: What is that to you? The King is up. When the King is
    awake, you are awake. Four o'clock. Six hours' sleep is
    enough for a man, seven for a woman, and eight for a fool.

FORTNUM: We've only had three. We didn't go to bed till one.

KING: Is that insolence, sir?

FORTNUM: No, sir. Arithmetic.
    *The* KING *tries to strike him.*

KING: What's your name?

FORTNUM: Fortnum, sir.

KING: Fetch me my breeches. Yours?

PAPANDIEK: You know my name, sir.

KING: Don't tell me what I know and don't know. What is it?

PAPANDIEK: Papandiek, sir. Arthur, sir.

KING: (*Peering at him*) Is it Arthur?

PAPANDIEK: Yes, sir.

KING: And yours?

BRAUN: Braun, sir.

KING: And yours?

FORTNUM: (*Wearily*) Fortnum, sir.

KING: Well, come on, boys, we're missing the best of the day.


EXT. WINDSOR TERRACE. DAY
*The* KING *hurries out on to the terrace, and then towards the park,*
*followed by the* PAGES.

KING: (*Singing*)
        Awake my soul and with the sun
        Thy daily stage of duty run
        Shake off dull sloth and joyful rise,
        To pay thy morning sacrifice.


EXT. WINDSOR PARK. THE FOLLY. DAY
*The* PAGES *pursue the* KING *through the morning mist as he runs past*
*a Gothick folly in the castle grounds.*

KING: Where's that other rascal, Braun? He's not gone back to
    bed?

BRAUN: (*Bringing a shirt*) I'm here, sir.

KING: Well give me my shirt, man. What shirt is this? It's calico.

Queen Charlotte, George III and Lady Pembroke

Sailcloth. It's a hairshirt. Fetch me another. Another shirt, lad, a softer shirt, a softer one.

INT. WINDSOR. LIVING-QUARTERS. DAY
BRAUN *banging on Greville's door.*
BRAUN: Wake up, sir. Attend, sir, attend.
    GREVILLE *put his head out from under the sheets.*

EXT. WINDSOR PARK. THE FOLLY. DAY
KING: Have you said your prayers this morning?
FORTNUM: I started, sir, but I was interrupted.
KING: Say after me – Our Father, which art in heaven, hallowed be Thy name, Thy kingdom come, Thy will be done, on earth as it is in heaven . . . (*etc.*)
    *The* QUEEN, LADY PEMBROKE *and* GREVILLE, *all in various stages of undress, come hurrying across the park, accompanied, immaculate as ever, by* FITZROY. *Seeing them, the* KING *continues to pray but takes the* QUEEN's *hand and makes her kneel down with them, kissing her hand repeatedly. Then he makes* LADY PEMBROKE *kneel, gazing fixedly at her before suddenly throwing himself onto her with passionate kisses.*

26

GREVILLE, *whose attention is as much on* LADY PEMBROKE *as the* KING, *puts an involuntary hand out to stop him.*

GREVILLE: Sir.

FITZROY: (*Outraged and slapping the hand down*) Sir!

*The* QUEEN *tries to pull the* KING *away from* LADY PEMBROKE.

QUEEN: Sir, we are in company.

KING: Mind your own business.

QUEEN: George!

FITZROY: The King has fallen. Help, sirs!

QUEEN: Help. Help the King. Help him. George.

LADY PEMBROKE: Sir. You must rest.

KING: I am the King. I cannot rest. I must rule.

*He finally breaks from her.*

Half the day gone already. There is much to do, there is government . . .

PAPANDIEK: Government hasn't begun yet, sir. Government is still in bed.

BRAUN: Government is lucky.


INT. WINDSOR. TERRACE. DAY

*The* KING *runs into the castle, pursued by the* PAGES.


INT. WINDSOR. LIVING-QUARTERS. CORRIDORS. DAY

*The* KING *in headlong flight, pursued by the* PAGES *and* GREVILLE *and gabbling all the time.*

KING: Do you love God, Arthur?

PAPANDIEK: Yes, sir.

KING: Oh, he loves you. He loves us all if only we will let him.

GREVILLE: Do not discuss the Deity, sir. It does not do.

*The* KING *rushes along a vaulted corridor and bursts into the room of a* LADY-IN-WAITING, *who is in bed.*

KING: Does not do? Does not do? I am the King. What is the Deity to me? Pisspot, pisspot.

*The* LADY *gives him the pot.*

LADY: Your Majesty.

KING: Do it, England! Do it. That's better. I am obliged to you, madam, Can't stop now. On, England, on!

*The* KING *hands back the chamber-pot to the startled* LADY-IN-

27

WAITING *and rushes away, followed by* GREVILLE *and*
PAPANDIEK. FORTNUM *politely relieves her of the (brimming)
receptacle and, mouthing a silent 'Thank you,' takes it outside,
where he runs into* BRAUN.

FORTNUM: Look, it's blue.

FITZROY: (*Coming round the corner*) What are you dawdling here
    for? The King is unattended.

FORTNUM: It's the King's water, sir. It's blue, sir.

FITZROY: So?

FORTUM: It's been this colour since this business began.

FITZROY: What business? Don't be insolent.

FORTNUM: We thought it might be important.

FITZROY: What is important is not to dangle about. Where is the
    King? Half undressed and unattended. That's what's
    important. Give me that.


INT. WINDSOR. CORRIDOR OUTSIDE KING'S APARTMENTS.
DAY

FITZROY *carries the chamber-pot along the corridor and encounters*
BAKER, *who is on his way to see the* KING.

FITZROY: Sir George . . . This is the King's water.

BAKER: Well?

FITZROY: It's blue.

BAKER: So?

FITZROY: It's been blue since His Majesty has been ill.

BAKER: Oh, God, another doctor. Medicine is a science. It
    consists of observation. Whether a man's water is blue or not
    is neither here nor there.
    *He goes into the anteroom, leaving* FITZROY *with the chamber-
    pot.*

FITZROY: (*Calling after* BAKER) Well, there's one blessing. At
    least he's stopped all the what, whatting.


INT. LIBRARY. NIGHT

GREVILLE, *exhausted and miserable, sits by the fire. He keeps
nodding off.* LADY PEMBROKE *comes in and watches* GREVILLE,
*amused that he is so sleepy. He struggles to his feet.*

GREVILLE: Lady Pembroke . . .

LADY PEMBROKE: Mr Greville. Her Majesty spoke favourably of

you today, Mr Greville. (*Conspiratorially*) And we do not like
Mr Fitzroy.
*She touches him on the arm and smiles.*
You will go far.


INT. WINDSOR. THE GREAT HALL. DAY
*Preparations for a concert.* FOOTMEN *are lighting candles in a huge
candelabra before hauling it up to the ceiling. Two large ceremonial
chairs on a dais in the centre of the hall face an orchestra, which is
already tuning up.*
PITT *and* DUNDAS, *both in topcoats, walk through the hall, where the
court is already assembled.* PITT *is plainly very cross.*
PITT: Captain Fitzroy! I said no concerts. No public appearances.
FITZROY: It's by order of the Prince. His Royal Highness thought
    it might cheer His Majesty up.
THURLOW: Come on, if we're late he will be mad.
    *Across the hall we see the* PRINCE OF WALES *with* DR
    WARREN.
PRINCE OF WALES: Do you like music, Warren?
WARREN: If it's played, sir, I listen to it.
PRINCE OF WALES: Soothes the savage breast, do you think?
WARREN: Not, I fear, in this case, sir.
    WARREN *permits himself a wintry smile.*


INT. WINDSOR. KING'S APARTMENTS. DUSK
*The* KING *has finished being attended to by* BAKER. PITT *has given
him some papers.*
KING: Push off, you fat turd.
BAKER: Yes, Your Majesty.
KING: What is this? (*Looking at the paper*) America, I suppose.
PITT: No, sir.
KING: Oh, America is not to be spoken of, is that it?
PITT: For your own peace of mind, sir. But it is not America.
    *The* KING *drops the paper.* PITT *desperately gives him another.
    And another. The* KING *takes no interest in them, dropping them
    or handing them to one of the* PAGES.
KING: Peace of mind! I have no peace of mind. I have had no
    peace of mind since we lost America. Forests, old as the
    world itself, meadows, plains, strange delicate flowers,

29

immense solitudes. And all nature new to art. All ours.
Mine. Gone. A paradise lost.

*Enter* FITZROY.

FITZROY: Her Majesty is waiting, sir.

PITT: I must ask you not to attend this concert, sir. You are not
fit, sir.

KING: Not fit?

PITT: To be seen, sir.

KING: Not fit?

PAGES: Sharp. Sharp. The King, the King.

KING: Not fit?

PITT: Sir, I beg you. I beg you, sir.

> PITT *loses all semblance of self-control and tries to prevent the*
> KING *leaving the room, but he is restrained by his colleagues and*
> *the* KING *strides into the concert in an extremely bad temper.*

INT. WINDSOR. THE GREAT HALL. DUSK

*A fanfare as the* KING *and* QUEEN *enter, the* KING *quite plainly not*
*fit to be seen, with stockings wrinkled and wig awry. The shock is seen*
*on the faces of the court as the royal couple move to their seats. There is*
*some craning of heads, some courtiers jumping on seats to try and catch*
*a glimpse of this wreck.*

KING: Not fit, not fit. I'll give him not fit. Telling me! I'm the
King, do you hear? The impudence. Well, I'm here now.
*The* KING *and* QUEEN *take their seats, but no sooner do they sit*
*down than the* KING *jumps up again and starts haranguing the*
*orchestra.*
Play, damn you. Play. Aha, remember this one? Louder,
sirs, louder, lay it on lads, one-two-three-four, one-two-
three-four. Come on, boys, let's hear you. Give it some stick.
You, put your heart into it, sir.
*He pushes the startled* HARPSICHORD PLAYER *off his seat, sits*
*down and starts playing.*
All right, move over. My turn. Where are we? Oh, yes, I see.
This is child's play, man. Oh, this is my favourite bit. That's
how to do it, see. Come on trumpets, give it some heart.

QUEEN: (*Coming up and whispering in the* KING's *ear*) Sir, you are
talking.

KING: I'm not, I'm playing.

30

QUEEN: But, sir . . .

KING: Not now, not now. Now give it a good whipping. Come on, come on. Thrash it, thrash it, you villains, what's the matter with you? Right.

*He gets up from the harpsichord, pointing out the place for the original* PLAYER, *who takes over again.*

There. Yes, this is Handel. I met him once. Ordinary-looking fellow. I have his harpsichord. All right then, let's be having you.

*He goes round the assembled company on* GREVILLE's *arm, peering into their faces.*

*Intercut in this scene with shots of various members of the court watching and whispering about the King, including the* PRINCE OF WALES, *who is urbane and unperturbed, and* MARIA FITZHERBERT, *who is alarmed and distressed.*

Elbow people. Knee gentlemen. Bending persons, handkissers.

*He stops in front of* LADY PEMBROKE, *and addresses his remarks about her to the* QUEEN, *who has followed him.*

*Looking at* LADY PEMBROKE's *breasts*:

Fine cluster there, eh?

*He gestures to the* QUEEN *to look.*

Go on, look, look. Go on. You might learn something. Good arse too, and warm, eh, I'll bet.

*He rubs his backside against hers and then moves on and stops in front of* MARIA FITZHERBERT. *He stares hard in her face, and then addresses the* PRINCE OF WALES.

What brings you to Windsor, sir?

PRINCE OF WALES: I had heard Your Majesty was indisposed. But I see . . .

KING: Indisposed!

PRINCE OF WALES: If there is any way I can assist . . .

KING: Want to hump the old bird out of the nest, is that it?

PRINCE OF WALES: (*Suddenly in earnest*) No, sir. There may be responsibilities that I could share . . .

KING: Want to get your fat hands on government, is that it?

*The* PRINCE OF WALES *shoots a look at* WARREN, *then at* MARIA FITZHERBERT.

Well, I am old and infirm. I shall not trouble you long.

31

PRINCE OF WALES: I wish you the best of health, father.

KING: Wish me, wish me? You wish me death, you plump little cuckoo.

PRINCE OF WALES: (*Laughing and pretending this is a joke*) Hush, father, hush.

KING: Hush? Hush? You dare to stop the King of England from speaking his mind. You powdered puppy.

*He turns away, then suddenly turns back and tries to throttle the* PRINCE OF WALES. *There is turmoil as the* PRINCE *turns to flee and the* KING *scrambles after him, jumping on his back and wrestling him to the ground.*

PRINCE OF WALES: Pa! Pa!

KING: I'll kill you. Choke the air out of you. Let me at him! I'll wring his neck.

QUEEN: (*Desperately*) It was something he ate.

*Father and son are separated and as the* KING *is helped out by* GREVILLE *and* FITZROY, *he shouts back.*

KING: You fools, can't you see that you will all be put out?

QUEEN: (*To* PRINCE OF WALES) We know your game, you monster.

*She follows.*

*Some of the* COURTIERS *crowd after the* KING *and* QUEEN, *some after the* PRINCE OF WALES.


INT. WINDSOR. DRAWING-ROOM. LATER. NIGHT

PITT, DUNDAS *and* THURLOW *are with the now-bandaged* PRINCE OF WALES. *Several* COURTIERS *look on, including* MARIA FITZHERBERT *and* FITZROY.

PRINCE OF WALES: As heir to the throne, Mr Pitt, I know that His Majesty bears a heavy burden. I fear the time is coming, Mr Pitt, when it is a burden we shall be forced to share.

PITT: Sir . . .

*He looks at* MARIA. *She half rises, is ready to go.*

PRINCE OF WALES: No, no, Mrs Fitzherbert has our entire confidence.

THURLOW *raises an eyebrow.* BAKER *comes in.*

Ah, Baker, how is the King?

BAKER: Still demented, sir, and the pulse is 104.

PRINCE OF WALES: Then he is not in command of his senses?

WARREN: Nor likely to be, if I may say so, sir.
PRINCE OF WALES: In that case, since His Majesty is not fit to look after himself, *we* must do so.
PITT *is alarmed.*
In the future, you – Warren – will partner Baker as the King's physician.
PITT: I must insist that this arrangement be subject to the approval of His Majesty's ministers.
PRINCE OF WALES: Insist? Approval? A son's concern for his sick father. What is the world coming to, Mr Pitt?
THURLOW: His Royal Highness is quite right. This is a family matter.
PRINCE OF WALES: Thank you, Lord Chancellor.

INT. WINDSOR. THE NURSERY. NIGHT
*The* KING, *now more dishevelled than ever, leads a train of* PAGES *and* EQUERRIES *as he stumbles round the castle, followed by the* QUEEN *and* LADY PEMBROKE.
KING: The children, the children!
QUEEN: The children are asleep, sir.
*We see three or four of them, sleeping in a large bed.*
KING: We must wake them. London is flooding. We must take the children and flee to higher ground. Save Amelia, Adolphus and little Octavius. Come, come, come . . .
*He picks up* AMELIA.
QUEEN: Octavius is dead, sir.
KING: Who killed him? His brother, the Prince of Wales? Yes, he would kill me too, I know.
*The* KING *rushes outside, clutching* AMELIA *and followed by the desperate* QUEEN, LADY PEMBROKE *and the* PAGES.

INT. WINDSOR. STAIRCASE TO ROOF. NIGHT
*The* KING *rushing up the staircase to the roof with* AMELIA.
KING: Hush, my baby. You're safe with Papa. Papa loves you, only he doesn't want you to get your feet wet, that's all. Come, come. But Papa's not mad, my darling. No, no. He has just lost himself, that's all. Hurry, we must get to the roof. We'll be safe up here, Amelia.

33

EXT. WINDSOR. ROOF. NIGHT

*They come out on to the roof. A surreal landscape of chimneys and castellations, windblown and lit by a full moon. As the* QUEEN *and the* PAGES *chase the* KING, *they look like an army of lunatics.*

QUEEN: Put her down, Sir, you are talking.

KING: I know I am talking. Do not tell me I talk. I follow my words. I run after them,. I am dragged at locution's tail. I have to talk in order to keep up with my thoughts.

AMELIA: I'm frightened.

KING: (*To* QUEEN) I thought he had taken you.

QUEEN: Who, sir?

KING: The other George. The fat one. You were not in my bed. I thought you had deceived me with the son.

QUEEN: Sir!

KING: Still, Elizabeth comes to my bed, don't you, Elizabeth?

QUEEN: Elizabeth, you leave us. All of you go, just go. Go, you too, go.

*The* QUEEN *wrests* AMELIA, *who is now hysterical, from the* KING, *puts her in someone's arms, and chases them all through the roof door. She turns to the* KING.

You want to talk? Well talk! Talk away!

KING: What do you do with him that you do not do with me, madam? At it like pigs, the pair of you, Huh? Those fat hands, that young belly. Your warm thighs. Harlot.

QUEEN: Be *still*, sir. For pity's sake. Listen. George. Hear me.

*She holds his mouth closed, and finally he is still.*

Do you think that you are mad?

KING: (*With sudden clarity, from the heart*) I don't know. I don't know. Madness isn't such torment. Madness is not half-blind. Madmen can stand. They skip! They dance! And I talk. I talk and talk and talk. I hear the words so I have to speak them. I have to empty my head of the words. *Something* has happened. *Something* is not right. Oh, Charlotte.

*They embrace, weeping in each other's arms.*


INT. WINDSOR. STAIRCASE TO ROOF. NIGHT

FITZROY, *pursued by* GREVILLE, *runs up a winding stair.*

GREVILLE: I will not do this, sir.

George III and Queen Charlotte

FITZROY: It is by order of the Prince.
GREVILLE: I am equerry to His Majesty, not the Prince.
FITZROY: His Majesty is out of his mind.

EXT. WINDSOR. ROOF. NIGHT
FITZROY *comes out on to the roof, followed by* GREVILLE.
QUEEN: Can we never be solitary? I told you to leave us. I am
    talking with His Majesty.
KING: Is it the floods? Have the waters spread?
QUEEN: Hush, George. Hush, George.
KING: No, no, no, my dear. Greville is right. He is right to take
    precautions. We must fetch the children. Take them to the
    higher ground. Save Amelia, Adolphus, little Octavius.
    Bring the Queen.
GREVILLE: Bring the Queen.
FITZROY: I have been instructed by His Royal Highness to move
    Your Majesty's lodgings, ma'am.
QUEEN: Why? Where?
FITZROY: It is to assist His Majesty's recovery.
GREVILLE: Captain Fitzroy.
FITZROY: Go, sir. *Go.*

GREVILLE *begins to lead the* KING *away, as* FITZROY *prevents the* QUEEN *from following.*

QUEEN: George!

FITZROY: Your Majesty is not to have access to the King's presence.

QUEEN: Not have access? But I am the Queen. Where are you taking him? No. No. Stop. George. Tyrant!
*The* KING *is taken away.*


INT. WINDSOR. PRINCE OF WALES'S ROOM. NIGHT
MARIA FITZHERBERT *quickly hides behind some other ladies as the* QUEEN *and* LADY PEMBROKE *burst in. The* QUEEN *advances smartly on the* PRINCE *and slaps his face.*

PRINCE OF WALES: Assaulted by both one's parents in the same evening! What is family life coming to?


INT. WINDSOR. ANTEROOM TO PRINCE OF WALES'S ROOM.
NIGHT
*The* COURTIERS *crowded at the door, giggling.*


INT. WINDSOR. PRINCE OF WALES'S ROOM. NIGHT
QUEEN: I was told it would be so. In England always the Prince hates the King.

PRINCE OF WALES: Is that why he is mad?

QUEEN: *If* he is mad, sir, you have made him so by your idleness.

PRINCE OF WALES: If I am idle, madam, it is because the King gives me nothing to do.

QUEEN: Do? Do what I do. I support him. I have his children. Fifteen of them.

PRINCE OF WALES: Then you should be grateful to me for giving you a breathing space . . . no, a breeding space. (*Trying not to laugh.*) I'm sorry, that really is awfully funny.
*The* QUEEN *looks around. Everyone is laughing. She breaks down.*

QUEEN: No, George, please. Please. Let me stay with him. Please, George.
*She is on her knees.*
*Cut away to* MARIA FITZHERBERT, *stopping her ears.*

PRINCE OF WALES: No, madam.

QUEEN: On what authority?

PRINCE OF WALES: On medical authority, ma'am. On the authority of a son, ma'am, who cares for his sick father.

QUEEN: But I am his wife. Do I not care for him too?

PRINCE OF WALES: Possibly, madam. But in his current frame of mind (*he looks at Lady Pembroke*) I'm afraid his Majesty does not seem to care for you.

QUEEN: Monster!

LADY PEMBROKE: Come, madam. Let me show Your Majesty where they have lodged us.

INT. MEDICAL AUDITORIUM. DAY

*An amputation is about to be performed, with* BAKER *and* PEPYS *among the small audience of physicians and surgeons watching.*

THURLOW *and* WARREN *come into the auditorium.*

*The* PATIENT *is strapped to the operating table and his gangrenous leg is exposed; the conversation between the* DOCTORS *is punctuated by the patient's screams.*

BAKER: This is Sir Lucas Pepys, Lord Chancellor, whom I have taken the liberty of consulting.

THURLOW: The more the merrier. Are you familiar with His Majesty's condition?

PEPYS: I have spent a lifetime in the study of the anfractuosities of the human understanding.

THURLOW: (*Irritably*) What?

PEPYS: The mind, sir, and its delinquencies. If it were possible, I would value an early view of one of His Majesty's motions.

THURLOW: Yes. That could be arranged, couldn't it? But what the devil is the matter with him?

BAKER: Persistent delirium. And the pulse sometimes rises to 110.

WARREN: Oh, the pulse varies. It doesn't signify.

PEPYS: I agree. I've always found the stool more eloquent than the pulse.

*The surgeons prepare to amputate.* THURLOW *pushes the* DOCTORS *towards the exit.*

THURLOW: So what do you suggest?

PEPYS: An immediate purge.

THURLOW: Warren?

WARREN: He needs blistering. Blistering on the back to draw the humours from the brain; blistering on the legs to draw the humours to the lower extremities.

*The* PATIENT *howls, out of view.*

BAKER: I agree, but he will never submit.

INT. WINDSOR. KING'S APARTMENTS. KING'S BEDROOM. DAY
*View of* BRAUN'S *legs coming into a room, seen from underneath the bed.*

*The* KING'S *hot face peering out.*

BRAUN: Hello there, Georgie boy.

WARREN, *the* PAGES, FITZROY *and* GREVILLE *come in.*

INT. WINDSOR. KING'S APARTMENTS. DRESSING-ROOM. DAY
*Cut to elaborately bandaged* KING, *bound to a bench, his arms pinioned to his side but his back and legs bare for blistering.*

*In desperation the* KING *prays aloud as* BRAUN *heats the glass cups over the flame from a spirit burner.*

KING: Not my skin, not my skin. Please. Oh, for pity's sake. No. I am the Lord's Anointed. O God, unto whom all hearts are open, all desires known, and from whom no secrets are hid, cleanse the thoughts of our hearts by the inspiration of Thy Holy Spirit that we may perfectly love thee and worthily magnify Thy holy name. Through Christ our Lord. Almighty and most merciful Father . . . We have erred and strayed from Thy ways like lost sheep. We have followed too much the devices and desires of our own hearts. Have mercy upon us, miserable offenders . . .

WARREN *now takes the heated cups and applies them to the* KING'S *back. The* KING *screams in agony and* GREVILLE *puts his hands over his ears.* FITZROY *is unmoved and helps hold the* KING *down.*

INT. WINDSOR. QUEEN'S LODGINGS. DAY
*The* QUEEN, *in her distant apartment, hears the King's screams.*

KING: Do not touch me, I'm the King. Go tell the Queen I am assaulted. The Queen, the Queen, help!

EXT. WINDSOR. THE TERRACE. DAY

PITT *and* FITZROY *alone. A cold day. Winter.*

FITZROY: He soils his clothes. Urine. Excrement. He talks filth.
The slops of his mind swilling over. I am not a nurse. If His
Majesty cannot regulate himself, how should he regulate the
country?

PITT *says nothing.*

I shall be relieved when it is ended . . . one way or another.

*The* KING *comes round a corner, helped by* GREVILLE, *followed
by the* PAGES. *He is wrapped in a rug, on his morning walk.*

KING: Arch-grand proprietor. Omni-felonious. Omni victorious,
happy and glorious.

FITZROY: Mr Pitt, Your Majesty.

KING: Where?

PITT: Here, Your Majesty.

KING: Stand close, Mr Pitt. You'll have to speak up, I don't see
very well. There is a fog here and in my ears – in my ears – in
my ears – ears . . .

PITT: There have been questions in the House, sir.

*This causes the* KING *to be suddenly lucid, though he quickly
loses control again.*

KING: Parliament . . . do nothing, Mr Pitt. I am not mad. I can't
see. There is a mist. Oh, the Queen, missed, oh, oh, missed
her, gone gone gone gone . . .

PITT: The doctors thought it best, sir.

KING: (*Instantly more agitated*) Doc doc doc doctors doctortures
doctormentors doctalk doctalk talk talk talk talk.

*The* KING *is howling helplessly and he takes* GREVILLE's *hand
and puts it over his mouth to stop him talking, while clutching his
incontinent behind and motioning them to take him away.*

GREVILLE: Come, sir, I'll hold you, sir, I'll hold you.

*To the distaste of* FITZROY *and the horror of* PITT, *the* KING
*lowers his breeches and squats miserably against the wall,
moaning to himself.* PITT *and* FITZROY *withdraw;* GREVILLE
*holds the* KING's *hand for a little while before he too withdraws
and the* KING *is left alone. Over this wretched, moaning figure
we hear, out of view, the imperturbable voice of* PITT *addressing
the House of Commons.*

PITT: (*Out of view*) Honourable members would, I am sure, like

39

to know that I saw His Majesty yesterday, and the only symptoms of his disorder were a tendency to repeat himself and a wandering from one topic to another . . . a characteristic that is shared by most of the converse of polite society, which if judged severely would warrant the consignment to Bedlam of many in this House.

INT. WESTMINSTER. HOUSE OF COMMONS. DAY
*Laughter.*
SPEAKER: Mr Fox.
FOX: Mr Pitt's consoling pleasantries should not deceive the
    House. The King is incapacitated.
    *Shouts of 'No, no.'*
    There are those who say he has lost his reason.
    *Uproar.*
    *Shouts of 'Nonsense,' 'No.'*
    In which case I propose that a Bill be drawn up to make the
    Prince of Wales Regent.
    *More uproar. Shouts of 'Close the doors.'*
SPEAKER: Order, order. The motion before this House is that a
    Bill be speedily drawn up to appoint the Prince of Wales
    Regent of this Kingdom. The House will divide.

INT. WESTMINSTER. HOUSE OF COMMONS. LOBBY. DAY
*The MPs are queuing up to vote.* FOX *is talking to the*
PRINCE OF WALES *and the* DUKE OF YORK.
FOX: Thank you, thank you, gentlemen. Sir, I must vote.
PRINCE OF WALES: Charles, for the life of me I can't see why
    they need to vote. The King is incapable. We know it. They
    know it.
    FOX *looks at the MPs waiting to vote.*
FOX: Sir. These are the nation's representatives. Now, some of
    them come to Parliament in the hope that they might serve
    their country, but most of them, being human, are here to fill
    their pockets. Pitt . . . and your father . . . have done them
    very well – pensions, places, bribes. But once it is plain that
    Pitt is finished and there is no more swill in the trough, Your
    Royal Highness will be made Regent. Sir, I must join the
    line.

The House of Commons

FOX *rushes over, his name is ticked off and he goes through the Lobby. There is a silence, followed a second later by a great shout. The* PRINCE OF WALES *and the* DUKE OF YORK *look delighted. The* DUKE OF YORK *shakes the* PRINCE'S *hand as MPs rush out of the chamber.* FOX *pushes through to the* PRINCE.
Rather good. Government majority of thirty.

PRINCE OF WALES: Government? Thirty?

DUKE OF YORK: You mean we haven't won?

FOX: Well, we didn't expect to win outright, not the first vote.

PRINCE OF WALES: I thought they liked me.

FOX: They will, sir, they will. In time.

PRINCE OF WALES: (*Furious*) Time, time, always time! *Now* is the time. Charles. *Now*!
*The Prince's fury briefly silences the hubbub in the Lobby as the* PRINCE *and the* DUKE OF YORK *sweep out.*

SHERIDAN: And that's our boy.

FOX: God rot all royals. Give us the wisdom of America.


EXT. WESTMINSTER. COURTYARD. DAY

PITT, DUNDAS *and* THURLOW *are parting. Other MPs also leaving the courtyard.*

DUNDAS: But he will recover in time . . . surely?

PITT: What good is that? Once he's made Regent the Prince will
have him locked away in some Windsor hellhole and mad or
sane no one will ever know.

THURLOW: You have been reading too many novels.

PITT: He has to recover soon or we are done for.

*As he leaves them,* PITT *is surprised to find* LADY PEMBROKE
*waiting in the cloisters.*

LADY PEMBROKE: Mr Pitt.

PITT: Lady Pembroke?

LADY PEMBROKE: Her Majesty understands that you are
dissatisfied with His Majesty's doctors.

PITT: The King is no better.

LADY PEMBROKE: Mr Pitt. My mother-in-law lost her wits, and a
succession of physicians failed to recover them for her. There
was, however, one doctor who was confident of her return to
health, and accordingly she was placed in his care.

PITT: And is she recovered?

LADY PEMBROKE: Entirely. Rides to hounds. Founded some
almshouses. Embroiders round the clock. I have written
down his name.

*She gives the note to* PITT.

EXT. LINCOLNSHIRE. DAY

*Against a flat Lincolnshire landscape silhouetted figures are engaged in
rustic tasks. They are smartly dressed and well above the general run of
farm labourers, genteelly (if somewhat ineffectually) tilling the soil.
Elegant women pick potatoes, gentlemen hoe, ladies rake . . . all under
the benevolent supervision of a severe figure in black:* DR WILLIS.

EXT. LINCOLNSHIRE. A FIELD. DAY

GREVILLE *picks his way across the field. Everyone turns and looks at
him. As he approaches* WILLIS, *a* LADY *drops her hoe and runs to
embrace him.*

MRS CORDWELL: At last! At last!

WILLIS: (*Reproving*) Mrs Cordwell.

MRS CORDWELL: This is my husband. Come post-haste from
Portsmouth.

*She puts her arm happily through* GREVILLE'*s.*

WILLIS: Mrs Cordwell. Captain Cordwell drowned off the
    Goodwins three years since.
MRS CORDWELL: (*Ruefully agreeing*) But he is very like.
WILLIS: Back to work, Mrs Cordwell.
    *She is led away.*
GREVILLE: Dr Willis?


EXT. WINDSOR. MAIN ENTRANCE. DAY
Willis's ATTENDANTS, *who are five heavy-set young men of brutal
appearance, unload some mysterious wooden sections from a cart.*


INT. WINDSOR. WALKING THROUGH KING'S APARTMENTS.
DAY
WILLIS: I must have certain undertakings. Authority over the
    patient. Access to him at all times.
PITT: You will reside here at Windsor. And Parliament will have
    to be kept informed, so you will need to write bulletins.
    They must be confident, optimistic. The survival of the
    Government depends upon it. And, Dr Willis, you are *my*
    doctor, do you understand?
WILLIS: I am the King's doctor, sir.
PITT: It is the same thing.
GREVILLE: (*Leading* WILLIS *away*) In here, sir.


INT. WINDSOR. KING'S APARTMENTS. ANTEROOM. DAY
Willis's ATTENDANTS, *carrying the wooden sections.*


INT. WINDSOR. KING'S APARTMENTS. DRAWING-ROOM. DAY
FOOTMEN *in attendance.* WILLIS *is examining the arrangements in
the King's apartments.*
WILLIS: Yes. Do you know, Mr Greville, the state of monarchy
    and the state of lunacy share a frontier. Some of my lunatics
    fancy themselves kings. He is the King so where shall his
    fancy take refuge?
GREVILLE: We do not use the word lunatic, sir, in relation to His
    Majesty.
WILLIS: Oh! Well, who is to say what is normal in a King?
    Deferred to, agreed with, acquiesced in. Who can flourish on
    such a daily diet of compliance? To be curbed, stood up to,

43

in a word thwarted, exercises the character, elasticates the spirit, makes it more pliant. It is the want of such exercise that makes rulers rigid.

PAGES: (*Out of view*) Sharp, sharp. The King, the King.

GREVILLE: This is the King, sir.

WILLIS: Whom I must cure.

*The* PAGES *bring in the* KING, *who talks all the time, very fast and without pause.*

*He is accompanied by* FITZROY *and a couple of* PAGES. *He sees* WILLIS *and slowly circles him, looking at him keenly but with no change in his tone.*

KING: . . . plough you a furrow as straight as a ruler, straight as a ruler done by a ruler. Ha! And another beside it and another beside that until you had as pretty a ploughed field as you could find this side of Cirencester. Put us out of our kingdom tomorrow and I would not want for employment.

WILLIS: (*Interrupts*) I have a farm.

KING: Give me the management of fifty acres and ploughing and sowing and harvest, and I could do it and make me a handsome profit into the bargain.

WILLIS: I said I have a farm, Your Majesty.

*The* KING *stops, looks at him, then starts talking again.*

GREVILLE: This gentleman, sir, has made the illness under which Your Majesty labours his special study.

KING: A mad doctor, is it? I am not mad, just nervous.

WILLIS: I shall endeavour to alleviate some of the inconveniences from which Your Majesty suffers.

KING: Inconveniences? Insults. Assaults. And salts beside rubbed into these wounds. Look.

*He tries to tear off the bandages.* WILLIS *examines the open wounds.*

By your dress, sir, and general demeanour, I would say you were a minister of God.

WILLIS: That is true, Your Majesty. I was once in the service of the Church. Now I practise medicine.

KING: Well, I am sorry for it. You have quitted a profession I have always loved, and embraced one I most heartily detest.

WILLIS: Our Saviour went about healing the sick.

KING: Yes, but he had not £700 a year for it.

44

GREVILLE *laughs; the* PAGES *laugh;* WILLIS *is unamused.*
Well, it's not bad for a madman.

WILLIS: I have a hospital in Lincolnshire.

KING: Lincolnshire, yes, I know Lincolnshire. Fine sheep there. Admirable sheep. Pigs, too. But I know of no hospitals.

WILLIS: My patients work, sir. They till the soil, and in so doing they acquire a better conceit of themselves.

KING: Well, I am King of England. A man can have no better conceit of himself than that.

WILLIS *takes hold of the* KING's *shoulder. The* KING *starts at the indignity and* GREVILLE *makes an involuntary movement of protest.* WILLIS *is not deterred and deliberately looks the* KING *in the eye.*
Do you look at me, sir?

WILLIS: I do, sir.

KING: I have you in my eye.

WILLIS: No. I have you in mine.

KING: You are bold, sir, but by God I am bolder.

*He attacks* WILLIS *as the* PAGES *rush forward to pull him back.* WILLIS *continues to look the* KING *in the eye.*
Do not look at me. I am not one of your farmers.

WILLIS: You must behave, or endeavour to do so.

KING: (*Still fighting*) Must, must. Whose must is this? Your must or my must? Get away from me, you scabby bum-sucker. Lincolnshire lickfingers.

WILLIS: Clean your tongue, sir. Clean your tongue.

KING: I will not. I will be a guest in the graveyard first.

WILLIS: Very well. If Your Majesty will not behave, you must be restrained.

*He opens the door to the anteroom, where his* ATTENDANTS *wait: brutal, unsmiling figures stood around a large wooden chair fitted with straps and a headrest. The* KING *falls silent looking at it.*

KING: When felons were induced to talk, they were shown first the instrument of their torture. The King is shown the instrument of his to induce him not to talk. Well, I won't, I won't, I won't.

45

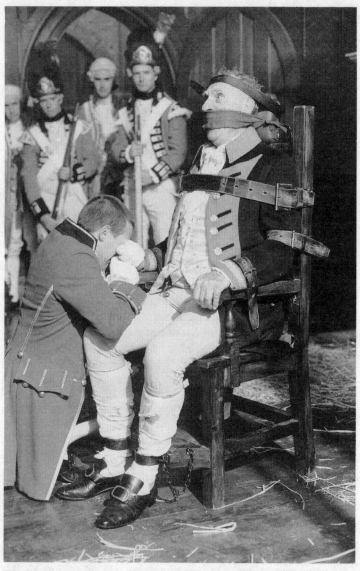

The King strapped in his restraining chair, his page Papandick at his feet

INT. WINDSOR. KING'S APARTMENTS. ANTEROOM. DAY
*Willis's* ATTENDANTS *seize the* KING, *to the consternation of the*
PAGES *and* EQUERRIES. *There is a struggle between the royal*
*retainers and Willis's* ATTENDANTS *in which the* ATTENDANTS *are*
*easily the winners, hurling the* PAGES *off and bloodying* GREVILLE's
*nose, while the* KING *tries to scramble away, shouting and screaming*
*obscenities. Eventually he is bundled into the chair and fastened in.*
WILLIS: Sit him down, sit him down.
   If the King refuses food, he will be restrained. If he claims to
   have no appetite, he will be restrained. If he swears and
   indulges in meaningless discourse, he will be restrained. If
   he throws off his bedclothes, tears away his bandages,
   scratches at his sores, and if he does not strive every day and
   always towards his own recovery, then he must be
   restrained.
   *The* KING *has been buckled into the chair and is helpless, a*
   *pathetic parody of the* KING *on his throne.*
KING: I am the King of England.
WILLIS: No, sir. You are the patient.
   *Underscoring the 'enthronement' in the restraining-chair is*
   *Handel's Coronation anthem 'Zadok the Priest', which, when*
   *the* KING *is bound and gagged and helpless, bursts forth at full*
   *volume.*


INT. WINDSOR. KING'S APARTMENTS. DAY
*Overhead shot of the* KING *struggling in the chair.*


EXT. WINDSOR CASTLE. DAY
*Faint lights in rooms; snow falling. Some servants scuttle across the*
*courtyard.*


INT. WINDSOR. QUEEN'S APARTMENTS. DAY
*The* QUEEN *is crouched over the fire, mittens on, while* LADY
PEMBROKE *indefatigably embroiders.*
QUEEN: Not permitted. Not permitted. We recommended him
   and still it's not permitted. None of them knows him.


INT. WINDSOR. QUEEN'S WINDOW. DAY
*She looks out of the window as the coach bearing* WARREN *and*

47

BAKER *arrives. We see them alight and go up the steps.*
WARREN: Come on, Baker, for heaven's sake.


INT. WINDSOR. QUEEN'S APARTMENTS. DAY
QUEEN: He is not himself. How can they restore him to his
    proper self not knowing what that self is?
    LADY PEMBROKE *embroiders on.*
    He is an angel of kindness and goodness.


INT. WINDSOR. KING'S APARTMENTS. BEDROOM. DAY
*Under Willis's paternal gaze, the* KING *hands his bedpan to*
FORTNUM. FORTNUM, *who has always been the prissiest of the*
*pages, takes it from the* KING *and without comment hands it to*
GREVILLE.
GREVILLE: (*Astonished at being given the bedpan*) Fortnum.
FORTNUM: Sir?
GREVILLE: What *are* you doing?
FORTNUM: I'm going, sir. To Piccadilly, sir. To start a provision
    merchant's. It isn't much, sir, but it's a cut above emptying
    pisspots.
    *He bows to the* KING *and goes out backwards.*
GREVILLE: (*Holding the bedpan out*) Braun.


INT. WINDSOR. KING'S APARTMENTS. DRAWING-ROOM. DAY
BRAUN *now takes the bedpan out to where* PEPYS *is waiting.* PEPYS
*takes it eagerly.*


INT. WINDSOR. KING'S APARTMENTS. ANTEROOM. DAY
PEPYS *puts the bedpan on a long table covered with chamber-pots and*
*the notebooks in which he has been recording the King's motions.*
WARREN *and* BAKER *come in.*
WARREN: Pepys?
PEPYS: Good news! A foetid and a stinking stool.
    (*He displays it.*)
    The colour good, well shaped and a prodigious quantity.
    Mind you, the urine is a little dark. Or is it the light?
WARREN: (*Motioning* PEPYS *out of the room, out of earshot of*
    *Willis's men*) Pepys!

The Doctors (*left to right*): Sir George Baker, Sir Lucas Pepys, Dr Richard Warren

INT. WINDSOR. CORRIDOR OUTSIDE KING'S APARTMENTS. DAY

WARREN: Pepys. This Willis.
PEPYS: Yes?
WARREN: A dangerous man.
PEPYS: Is he?
WARREN: Not a proper doctor.
BAKER: Not a member of the Royal College of Physicians.
WARREN: Wants us out, Pepys.
PEPYS: No!
WARREN: We must stick together. And remember: one voice.
PEPYS/BAKER: One voice.

INT. CARLTON HOUSE. DRAWING-ROOM. NIGHT

MARIA FITZHERBERT *embroidering*. PRINCE OF WALES *and* WARREN *perambulating*, PRINCE *looking grave*.

PRINCE OF WALES: What kind of fellow is he?
WARREN: Parson. Quack. Has some modern ideas. He'll need watching.
*They exchange looks.*

49

MARIA: I've heard very good things about him. They say he does a lot of it with his eyes.
PRINCE OF WALES: You mean he *looks* at the King?
WARREN: Yes.
PRINCE OF WALES: Damned impudence.
MARIA: (*Artlessly, and as ever trying to reconcile father and son*) Poor King. And no Queen. He must be very lonely. It's such a pity he's not nearer, then you could go visit him.
*The* PRINCE *looks at her thoughtfully.*
PRINCE OF WALES: Ye-es.
WARREN: You don't mean . . . here?
PRINCE OF WALES: Good God, no. Kew.


EXT. WINDSOR. COURTYARD. DAY
*The* KING, *dressed only in his nightshirt and a straitjacket, is dragged across the snow-covered courtyard towards a waiting carriage. He is shouting and struggling.*


INT. WINDSOR. QUEEN'S APARTMENTS. DAY
*The* QUEEN, *hearing the commotion, goes to the window. She is horrified.*


EXT. WINDSOR. COURTYARD. DAY
WILLIS: (*Fixing the* KING *with his eye*) I see you, sir.
KING: No, sir. You do not see me. Nobody sees me. I am not here. (*To his captors who are dragging him to the coach.*) Get your filthy hands off me, you . . .


INT. WINDSOR. QUEEN'S APARTMENT. DAY
*The* QUEEN *watches as . . .*


EXT. WINDSOR. COURTYARD. DAY
*The* KING *breaks away from his captors but is caught again.*


EXT. WINDSOR. COURTYARD. DAY
WILLIS: I have you in my eye, sir, and I shall keep you in my eye until you learn to behave and do as you are told.
KING: I am the King. I tell. I am not told. I am the verb, sir. I am not the object.
WILLIS: Until you can govern yourself, you are not fit to govern

others, and until you do so I shall govern you.

KING: Govern yourself, then, you goat.

*He blows a raspberry at* WILLIS.

WILLIS: Get him in the coach.

*The* KING *is heaved, struggling, into the coach.*

KING: Then I am dead. I am a coffin king. I shall be taken out, murdered and my genitals torn off and pulled apart by horses and my limbs exhibited in a neighbouring town. Help me, please, help me.


EXT. WINDSOR. COURTYARD. DAY

*The* QUEEN *and* LADY PEMBROKE *rush out to see coach departing.*


EXT. WINDSOR. COURTYARD. DAY

*The* QUEEN *runs alongside the coach.*

QUEEN: Mr King.


INT. CARRIAGE. DAY

*The* KING *is sitting by the window,* FITZROY *beside him, opposite him* GREVILLE *and one or two of Willis's* ATTENDANTS. *The* KING *stares out at the* QUEEN. *The* QUEEN *stares at the* KING.


EXT. KEW. PALACE. DAY

*The coach arrives at Kew. It is snowing. The exterior of the house is cold, forbidding and doom-laden.*


INT. KEW. ENTRANCE HALL. DAY

*The* KING *is carried up the steps while in his restraining chair, and then indoors.*


INT. KEW. DRAWING-ROOM. NIGHT

*It is so cold one of the* PAGES *grabs a dustsheet from a statue to wrap round the* KING.

KING: The Queen will be at Kew, you said.

WILLIS: She will, sir, in time.

KING: It was a lie. You are an ordained minister and you told me a lie. Well, that lie will have you out of that famous farm of yours and loose your tame lunatics across Lincolnshire. You liar! Liar!

51

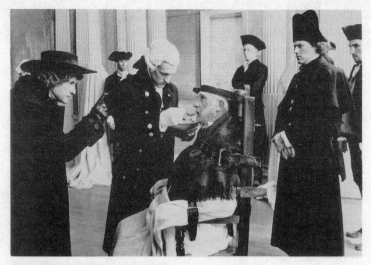
Dr Willis, Papandiek, George III and Captain Greville

INT. KEW. DRAWING-ROOM. NIGHT
*A plate of soup is brought to* WILLIS, *who feeds the* KING *with a spoon.* WILLIS *forces the* KING *to look at him as he holds a spoonful of soup, which he puts into the* KING'S *mouth. The* KING *looks at him boldly. Then spits the soup out in* WILLIS'S *face.* WILLIS *is unmoved, and feeds him some more. The* KING *is about to spit it out again but Willis's look stops him.* WILLIS *turns away and the* KING, *glowering, swallows it.*

INT. KEW. DINING-ROOM. DAY
*The* KING, *now formally dressed in black, sits at a table, with* WILLIS, *the* PAGES, FITZROY *and* GREVILLE *looking on.*
KING: I'm here, but I'm not all there.
        *The* KING *eats, feeding himself. All begin to applaud.*

INT. KEW. DINING-ROOM. DAY
*The* KING *drawing,* WILLIS *sitting by him. He is drawing a picture of* WILLIS.
WILLIS: (*Looking at the picture*) Ye-es.
        *He pins it on the wall.*

Dr Willis, Prime Minister Pitt and Lord Chancellor Thurlow

EXT. KEW. DAY
*The* KING *sits in the grounds with* PAPANDIEK. *The* KING, *cloaked and bearded now, looks like Lear.*

INT. KEW. DRAWING-ROOM. DAY
WILLIS *is watching the previous scene through the window.*
PITT: (*Out of view*) I used to sit with my father when he was ill.
    *We pull out to find that* PITT *and* THURLOW *are now with*
    WILLIS.
    I used to read him Shakespeare.
WILLIS: I have never read Shakespeare.
    PITT *looks at him somewhat askance.*
    I am a clergyman.

EXT. KEW. MAIN ENTRANCE. DAY
WILLIS *is waiting on the steps of the house with* PITT *and*
THURLOW. *Seeing them, the* KING *is nervous and dismayed, his step falters and, though* PAPANDIEK *takes his arm, his confidence has plainly gone and he reverts to his old state.*
KING: They have killed the Queen. Did you know that?
PITT: No, sir.
KING: Ah, yes, sir. Are you cold?
THURLOW: It is chilly, sir.
KING: Not for me. I make the weather by means of mental
    powers.
    *They go inside.*

INT. KEW. ENTRANCE HALL. DAY
KING: Well, actually, actually it is not too bad about the Queen,
    because actually I was never actually married to her. I was
    married to the tall one, Elizabeth. *Sie öffnet ihre Beine zu*
    *jeder Zeit wenn ich es will. Vier, fünf Mal am Tag, wie mich die*
    *Laune trift.*
WILLIS: What are you saying, sir?
KING: Oh, do they not speak German in Lincolnshire? Then
    allow me to translate, sir. Her ladyship is game for it any
    time. I just have to say the words and her skirt's up, legs in
    the air . . . I just tip her the wink and I'm in there. Or she's
    down here.

WILLIS: Gag!

> The KING *is gagged and Willis's* ATTENDANTS *drag him away cursing.*

PITT: You assured me you could cure him.

WILLIS: I can, sir, given time.

PITT: We do not have time.

INT. CARLTON HOUSE. PRINCE OF WALES'S BEDROOM. NIGHT
MARIA FITZHERBERT *is kneeling at the altar. The* PRINCE OF WALES *is watching her.*

PRINCE OF WALES: What are you praying for now?

MARIA: The King.

PRINCE OF WALES: You should pray for us, because if he did die, or stay mad . . .

MARIA: George!

PRINCE OF WALES: . . . what is to stop us saying we are man and wife? Huh?

INT. A CHURCH VESTRY. DAY
THURLOW *is interviewing a shabby and bibulous* CLERGYMAN.

THURLOW: Didn't you know who the bridegroom was?

CLERGYMAN: (*Looking through a parish register*) It's a year or two ago.

THURLOW: And did the bride not mention she was a Catholic?

CLERGYMAN: (*Shakes his head*) Why should she? Ah, here it is.

THURLOW: (*Looking at the entry*) The Prince cannot marry without the King's permission. And he cannot marry a Catholic. You performed an illegal marriage.

CLERGYMAN: And he only gave me £10!

THURLOW: Here is £10 more. Keep your mouth shut.

> THURLOW *rips the page out of the register.*

CLERGYMAN: Here, that's against the law.

THURLOW: I am the law.

INT. WINDSOR. QUEEN'S APARTMENTS. NIGHT
*The* QUEEN *is sitting at her dressing-table, preparing for bed,* LADY PEMBROKE *standing by her side.*

QUEEN: Oh, long, long days, Elizabeth.

> LADY PEMBROKE *smiles, sadly.*

LADY PEMBROKE: And longer for His Majesty.

INT. KEW. ENTRANCE HALL. DAY
*The three* DOCTORS *bustle in from the cold outside.*
FITZROY: In the drawing-room, gentlemen.


INT. KEW. DRAWING-ROOM. DAY
FITZROY: The doctors, Your Majesty.
BAKER: Good-afternoon, Your Majesty. And how are we today?
    *The* KING *says nothing, sulking.* WARREN *examines his head,*
    *while* BAKER *reads the bulletin.*
WARREN: The blisters have healed up very nicely. Which won't do
    at all.
    *He forces them open again with his fingers. The* KING *screams out.*
    GREVILLE *and* PAPANDIEK *turn away in disgust.*
KING: Get off me, you barbarian.
    WILLIS *looks reprovingly at the* KING, *who sighs and goes over to*
    *the restraining-chair, where he allows himself to be gagged and*
    *strapped in.*
WILLIS: (*Handing* WARREN *the bulletin*) Bulletin.
WARREN: (*Reading*) Much better? Well, I can't see it.
WILLIS: Do you doubt my word, sir?
WARREN: (*Screwing up the paper*) I'll write it.
PEPYS: Could we mention the stool this time?
WARREN: (*Writing*) Oh, the stool, the stool. My dear Pepys, the
    persistent excellence of the stool has been one of this disease's
    most tedious features. When will you get it into your head that
    one can produce a copious, regular and exquisitely turned
    evacuation every day of the week and still be a stranger to
    reason?


INT. HOUSE OF COMMONS. DAY
*Close-up on the bulletin.* PITT *has it on the dispatch box in front of him.*
*The* PRINCE OF WALES *and* WARREN *sitting smugly in the gallery.*
PITT: Mr Speaker. I will not trouble the House with the detailed
    contents of the latest – and I may say generally optimistic –
    bulletin, but honourable members would, I am sure, like to
    know that while His Majesty has had his ups and downs, his
    health continues . . . steadily to improve.
    FOX *is on his feet. The* PRINCE OF WALES *and* WARREN *are*
    *outraged.*

WARREN: Barefaced lie!

FOX: Ups and downs? Ups and downs? Mr Speaker, I can – with your permission – quote from a copy of the same bulletin handed to me by Dr Warren. Some of these 'ups and downs': His Majesty's obscenities; his blasphemies; his interminable ramblings . . .

*Uproar.*

Suffice it to say that this optimistic bulletin concludes thus: that while His Majesty has had lucid intervals, he remains periodically demented and incapable of rational thought.

*In the gallery the* PRINCE OF WALES *nods in approval.*


INT. KEW. DINING-ROOM. DAY

*This and the following scene are intercut between Kew and the House of Commons. At Kew preparations are being made to shave the* KING. *As bowls of water and a shaving brush are placed on the table, we see behind him rows of drawings, all dated and pinned to the wall.*

PAPANDIEK *clips the King's beard before sharpening the razor.*

FOX: I put it to the House that we have been deceived too long over His Majesty's continuing illness. When are we going to see the Bill appointing the Prince Regent?

*The* KING *regards himself in the mirror, then reaches for the razor with* WILLIS, GREVILLE, FITZROY *and the* PAGES *all watching him. The* KING *makes a sudden movement with the razor, as if he's going to attack them.* BRAUN *jumps back. The* KING *laughs.*

MPS: (*Out of view*) When? When?

PITT: In due course. It is still being drafted.

*More shouts of 'When?'*

SPEAKER: Order, Order!

PITT: Soon.

*Uproar. The faces of the MPs in close-up are madder than the King's ever was.*

SPEAKER: Order, order. On Mr Fox's motion to present the Bill, the House will divide. Ayes to the right, nos to the left.

*The* KING *proceeds to shave himself perfectly.*


INT. WESTMINSTER. HOUSE OF COMMONS. LOBBY. DAY

*The sound of cheering from the Chamber as* DUNDAS *pushes through to* PITT *and* THURLOW.

DUNDAS: They won. Just three votes.

THURLOW: Then you must present the Bill. The Prince must be made Regent.


INT. A CHURCH. DAY

FOX *and* SHERIDAN *sitting in a pew.* FOX *impatiently looking at his watch.* THURLOW *comes in with exaggerated stealth and takes the pew behind them, kneeling down and holding the bridge of his nose fastidiously between thumb and forefinger.*

FOX: Well?

THURLOW: I'm praying, goddamn it.

> *He finishes praying.*

I'm almost ready to give you my support.

FOX: Now? We don't need you now.

THURLOW: I think you do.

> *He hands* FOX *the page torn from the marriage register.*

Your boy's married.

FOX: No. She's just his mistress.

> *He looks at the page.*

THURLOW: I haven't told Mr Pitt. Yet.

SHERIDAN: What is it you want?

THURLOW: The good of the country.

> FOX *snorts contempuously.*

To remain as Lord Chancellor.


INT. CARLTON HOUSE. DINING-ROOM. DAY

THURLOW, FOX *and* SHERIDAN *are now at dinner with the* PRINCE OF WALES, MARIA *and* WARREN.

PRINCE OF WALES: Well, I'm sure that can be arranged. When, and if, we ever manage to get our hands on government.

> *The* PRINCE *glares at* FOX.

FOX: The Bill is ready, sir.

PRINCE OF WALES: I am a snail, Lord Chancellor, creeping my way towards the throne. Even Maria is becoming impatient.

MARIA: Only for His Majesty's recovery, sir.

FOX: And now the Lord Chancellor has come out in favour of your Royal Highness, the end is surely in sight.

THURLOW: I have always been in favour of His Royal Highness.

FOX: Of course.

58

The Prince of Wales

THURLOW: Though I would say the present situation calls for a certain delicacy.

MARIA: (*To* PRINCE OF WALES) This is your father, sir. Be kind.

THURLOW: Lie on your oars, sir, the tide is with you.

PRINCE OF WALES: (*Fuming*) The tide? Lie on my oars?

MARIA: George!

THURLOW: Your Royal Highness has but to wait.

PRINCE OF WALES: Wait! Wait! Lord Chancellor, my life has been waiting. I endeavour to cultivate languor. But it is difficult to be languid when the throne of England is pending. People laugh at me. What must I do to be taken seriously? I tell you, sir, to be Prince of Wales is not a position. It is a predicament.

*He gathers up* MARIA *and leaves.*

FOX: She has more sense than he has.

THURLOW: It takes character to withstand the rigours of indolence.


INT. WESTMINSTER. HOUSE OF COMMONS. DAY
*The Regency Bill being distributed at the House of Commons. MPs reading it.*


INT. CARLTON HOUSE. DRAWING-ROOM. DAY
THURLOW *has brought the* PRINCE OF WALES *a copy of the Regency Bill. The* PRINCE *reads it, looking for some mention of his wife.*

PRINCE OF WALES: Maria is not mentioned.

THURLOW: No, sir. It's a little early for that.

PRINCE OF WALES: It will happen, Maria, I promise you. Won't it, Thurlow?

THURLOW: Sir.

*It is plain that he doesn't think so, and nor does she.*


INT. WINDSOR. QUEEN'S APARTMENTS. DAY
*The* QUEEN *is reading over the Bill.*

QUEEN: No, no. This must not be, the son in charge of the father. He will be put away. This is his death warrant. Elizabeth. I must see him. Elizabeth!

*Close-up on* LADY PEMBROKE, *who knows what is expected of her. She collects her cloak and makes to leave.*

60

INT. KEW. GREVILLE'S ROOM. DAY
LADY PEMBROKE *is sitting.* GREVILLE *is standing. She has just finished explaining her request.*
GREVILLE: I cannot do it, ma'am.
> LADY PEMBROKE *gets up.*
> Besides, if Her Majesty sees him . . . he . . . he . . . he . . . still . . . utters such improprieties.
> LADY PEMBROKE *smiles at his confusion.*
LADY PEMBROKE: What about?
GREVILLE: About . . . about you, madam.
LADY PEMBROKE: Tell me.
GREVILLE: I cannot say.
LADY PEMBROKE: What is it His Majesty dreams of doing, Mr Greville?
> *She has him backed up against the door.*
> Is it this?
> *She takes* GREVILLE's *hand and puts it on her breast.*
> GREVILLE *shakes his head helplessly.*
> This? Or this?
> *Her left hand goes down out of frame and* GREVILLE *catches his breath.* GREVILLE *dissolves into a kiss, out of control.*
> LADY PEMBROKE *is perfectly in control.*

INT. KEW. STAIRCASE. DAY
*The* KING's *delighted face, as he and the* PAGES *slide down the banisters. The* KING *is well shaved and looks healthy and* WILLIS *seems in good spirits.* BAKER *and* FITZROY, *on the other hand, are disdainful.*
KING: Come on, lads! Race you to the door. Come on . . . I won!

INT. KEW. ENTRANCE HALL. DAY
BAKER *is leaving.* KING, WILLIS, FITZROY *and the* PAGES *see him off.*
KING: (*Winking at the* PAGES) Oh, Baker. Baker, before you leave . . .
BAKER: Sir?
KING: I have a little job for you. A secret mission.
BAKER: Yes, sir.
KING: Yes. I want you to hand over Gibraltar to Spain and see if you can get Minorca in return. Now, do you think you could

61

do that?

BAKER: I'm a physician, sir.

KING: Then you should have no difficulty. Good afternoon.

> BAKER *shakes his head at* WILLIS *and goes out. With more whoops of delight, the* KING *gives* PAPANDIEK *a piggyback and runs with him into the drawing-room.*

INT. KEW. DRAWING-ROOM. DAY

*Where he is suddenly confronted by the* QUEEN. *Silence.* FITZROY *glares at* GREVILLE, *who plainly is responsible for the visit.*

QUEEN: Your Majesty.

> *The* KING *appears to ignore her, and sits down.*

Have you nothing to say to me, sir?

KING: Say, madam? What is there to say? We were married for twenty-eight years, never separated even for a day, yet you abandoned me to my tormentors.

QUEEN: The doctors said it was for your good.

KING: My good? What do they know of my good?

QUEEN: George. They may not permit me to see you again. A Bill has been prepared to make the son Regent.

KING: (*Laughing incredulously*) Regent?

QUEEN: (*Producing the Bill*) Do you understand? He is to rule in your place.

KING: Regent? The fat one?

FITZROY: His Majesty has not been told about the Bill, madam.

QUEEN: He must know. George, you must know. He must know. Do you understand? The son.

FITZROY: Come away, madam. Come away.

> *He pushes the* QUEEN *out of the room.*

KING: The son! The father pushed aside, put out, put away. Ruled out. The father not dead even. By whose authority? (*Reading*) 'The Prince of Wales should have full power and authority' . . . 'All authorities, prerogatives.' Why was I not told of this?

> PAPANDIEK *tries to calm and restrain him, but the* KING *pushes him violently to the floor and tries to run after the* QUEEN.

WILLIS: (*Taking the Bill from him*) The Bill doesn't matter, sir.

GREVILLE: (*Desperately*) Your Majesty, this Bill is to be presented today, sir. The Prince of Wales has a majority in the House.

WILLIS *looks at the* KING *and the* KING *straight away calms down.*

KING: Greville! Dr Willis is right. Take it away.


INT. WESTMINSTER. LOBBY. DAY

*MPs are thronging into the House.* FITZROY *forces his way through the crowds to where the* PRINCE OF WALES *and the* DUKE OF YORK *are standing with* WARREN *and* FOX. FITZROY *whispers in the* PRINCE's *ear.*

DULE OF YORK: What's that? He's on the mend? I say, that's good news!

PRINCE OF WALES: Does anyone else know?

> FITZROY *shakes his head.*

FITZROY: No, sir.

WARREN: It may be only temporary.

> FITZROY *doesn't say anything to encourage this.*

PRINCE OF WALES: Well, I see no reason to disseminate the information. We can decide how ill His Majesty is when the Bill is passed, eh, Warren?

> *They are about to go into the Gallery.*

Nearly there, Charles.

> FOX *looks unhappy.*

FOX: Where's Thurlow?


INT. KEW. UNDER A TREE. DAY

THURLOW *approaching. The* KING *and* WILLIS *reading.*

WILLIS: 'These weeds are memories of those worser hours . . .'

KING: 'I prithee put them off.' Go on man, go on.

WILLIS: 'I prithee put them off.'

KING: 'How does the King?'

WILLIS: 'How does the King?'

> WILLIS *is obviously no actor.*

PAPANDIEK: Lord Thurlow, sir.

THURLOW: Your Majesty.

KING: Ah, Thurlow. The very man. Yes, we are reading a spot of Shakespeare. Willis, give him the book.

THURLOW: (*Sotto voce to* WILLIS) King Lear? Is that wise?

WILLIS: I'd no idea what it was about.

KING: I'm asleep apparently and Cordelia comes in and asks the doctor – that's Greville here – how I am, you see. Off we go.

THURLOW: Who's Cordelia?

KING: You are. Yes, but . . . Willis can't do it. He's a fine doctor, but a hopeless actor. Off you go.

THURLOW: (*As Cordelia*)
    'O you kind gods
    Cure this great breach in his abused nature.
    Th'untuned and jarring senses, O wind up,
    Of this child-changed father.'

KING: That's very good. 'Child-changed father''s very good. Go on, Greville, it's you now.

GREVILLE: 'He hath slept long, be by, good madam, when we do awaken him. I doubt not of his temperance.'

THURLOW:
    'O my dear father! Restoration hang
    Thy medicine on my lips, and let this kiss
    Repair those violent harms which my two sisters
    Have in thy reverence made.'

KING: Well, come on, man. Come on. Kiss me.

    THURLOW *goes for the* KING'*s hand.*

KING: No, not there, man. Here. Here. It's Shakespeare. Right. *Gives him his cheek to kiss.*
Now, push off again. This is the moment when the King awakes, you see. Are you ready? That's it, come on.
*The* KING *does an elaborate and old-fashioned pantomime of waking up.*

THURLOW: 'How fares my Royal Lord? How does your Majesty?'

KING: (*As Lear*)
    'You do me wrong to take me out o' th' grave.
    Thou art a soul in bliss, but I am bound
    Upon a wheel of fire, that mine own tears
    Do scald like molten lead.'
Oh, it's so true!
    'Pray do not mock me.
    I am a very foolish, fond old man.
    And, to deal plainly,
    I fear I am not in my perfect mind.'

WILLIS: Is that the end, Your Majesty?

KING: Oh, good Lord no . . . Cordelia – that's Thurlow – dies.

64

Thurlow, Dr Willis, George III and Captain Greville reading *King Lear*

Hanged. And the shock of it kills the king. So they all die.
It's a tragedy.

THURLOW: (*Moved*) Very affecting.

KING: Well, it's the way I play it.

THURLOW: Your Majesty seems more yourself.

KING: Do I? Yes, I do. I have always been myself even when I
was ill. Only now I seem myself. That's the important thing.
I have remembered how to seem. What, what?

GREVILLE *starts.*

GREVILLE: What did Your Majesty say?

KING: What? I didn't say anything. Besides, Greville, you're not
supposed to ask the King questions, you should know that.
What, what?

THURLOW, *in close-up, recognizes what the 'What, What?'
signifies.* GREVILLE *breaks into a broad smile.*

THURLOW: Get him ready.

EXT. KEW. LAKE. DAY

BRAUN *and* PAPANDIEK *carrying chamber-pots to the lake.*

BRAUN: Here, look at his piss. We're back to lemonade.

PAPANDIEK: No. Mine's still a bit inky.

BRAUN: But that's yesterday's. This is today's. Here, Piss the
     Elder! Piss the Younger!
     *They both laugh. They pour the piss into the lake in two brightly
     coloured streams.*


EXT. KEW. FRONT STEPS. DAY
*The King's coach leaves Kew.*


INT. WESTMINSTER. HOUSE OF COMMONS. DAY
*The* PRINCE OF WALES *coming into the gallery, acknowledging the
cheers of the MPs.*
SPEAKER: The matter before this House is a Bill to provide for the
     care of His Majesty's Royal person and for the
     administration of the Royal authority during the continuance
     of His Majesty's illness.


EXT. CHISWICK. LONDON ROAD. DAY
*Shots of Thurlow's coach going hell for leather.*


INT. WESTMINSTER. HOUSE OF COMMONS. DAY
MP: Mr Speaker. We on this side of the House count ourselves
     fortunate that we have in the person of the Prince of Wales a
     young man of such character and aptitude . . .


EXT. LONDON ROAD. DAY
THURLOW *looking out of his coach, which is now surrounded by
sheep, baa-ing (not unlike the MPs).*
THURLOW: God's teeth. What now?


INT. WESTMINSTER. HOUSE OF COMMONS. DAY
FOX *is brandishing a list of reforms he intends to bring in.*
FOX: And so, Mr Speaker, I would like to set out some measures
     of long-overdue reform and, yes, I make bold to say it,
     necessary expenditure, that when His Royal Highness is
     declared Regent . . .
     *Cheers.*
     PITT *and* DUNDAS *on the front bench, looking glum.*


66

EXT. WESTMINSTER. COURTYARD. DAY
*The coach rattles into the yard.* THURLOW *staggers out of the coach (windows still curtained) and rushes into the Palace, sending an* ATTENDANT *to fetch* PITT *from the Commons.*

INT. WESTMINSTER. HOUSE OF COMMONS. DAY
*A note is passed to* PITT, *who hurriedly leaves the House with* DUNDAS.

INT. WESTMINSTER. LOBBY. DAY
THURLOW: I've just been with His Majesty and have had two
    hours' uninterrupted conversation with him.
DUNDAS: Oh, God, you mean he's talking again?
THURLOW: No, damn it. Well, yes. But not fifty to the dozen,
    and not nonsense either. He's actually a damned clever
    fellow. Had me reading Shakespeare. Have you read *King
    Lear*? Tragic story. Of course, if that fool of a messenger had
    just got that little bit more of a move on, Cordelia wouldn't
    have been hanged, Lear wouldn't have died, and it would all
    have ended happily . . . which I think would have made a
    much better ending. Because as it is, it's so damned
    tragic . . .
DUNDAS: Lord Chancellor . . .
THURLOW: The point is, the King is better.
PITT: Better than he was?
THURLOW: No. Better. The 'what, what?' is back, the 'hey, hey'.
    Come.
    *Incredulity on* PITT'*s and* DUNDAS'*s faces as they follow*
    THURLOW *down the corridor, gradually breaking into a run.*

INT. WESTMINSTER. HOUSE OF COMMONS. DAY
*An MP is on his feet speaking.*
MP: No one, Mr Speaker, entertains a higher regard for His
    Majesty than I do. But we cannot close our eyes to the fact
    that His Majesty has been overtaken by a terrible and, I fear,
    long-lasting illness that seems immune to all forms of
    medical treatment.
    *As he drones on, we see the word pass along the benches that the*
    KING *is outside and MPs begin to leave rapidly.* FOX *stands up
    and looks over to the gallery, where the* PRINCE OF WALES, *not*

*having heard the news, is puzzled. Then someone whispers to him
and he too rushes out.*

INT. WESTMINSTER. HOUSE OF COMMONS LOBBY. DAY
*Pandemonium as MPs rush through the Lobby, pushing and shoving
and trying to get out into the courtyard, the* PRINCE OF WALES *and*
FOX *among them.*

EXT. WESTMINSTER. COURTYARD. DAY
*As the MPs spill out into the courtyard we see the curtains of the coach
drawn back.* THURLOW *opens the door and* WILLIS *comes round to
hand out the* KING.
*The* PRINCE OF WALES *forces his way through the crowd and shrinks
back in despair at the sight of the recovered* KING, *who is just
gathering himself together before he addresses the MPs, now suddenly
silent, waiting to see if he is indeed better.*
KING: (*Haltingly, but with growing confidence*) I . . . we . . . are
    touched by the concern shown by our most loyal subjects and
    are very happy to be amongst you all again. Be assured that
    now that our strength has returned, we will once more take
    up the reins of government.
    *A pause. The courtyard erupts to shouts of 'Long live the King',
    etc. The* KING *turns to* WILLIS.
    How was that, lads? Not bad, eh, what, what?
    *The* KING *is surrounded by jubilant MPs, as the* PRINCE OF
    WALES *swoons.*

EXT. WINDSOR. COURTYARD. DAY
*The King's carriage arrives back at Windsor as all the* CASTLE
SERVANTS *cheer.*
PAPANDIEK: Your Majesty! Sharp, sharp. The King, the King.
ALL: The King, The King!
AMELIA: Papa, Papa!
KING: Oh, Amelia.
ADOLPHUS: Pa, you're back, you're back. Come with me, come
    with me, Mama is in the garden.

EXT. WINDSOR. TERRACE/GARDEN. DAY
*We see the* QUEEN *approach the* KING, *curtsy and kiss his hand.*

68

The Duke of York and the Prince of Wales

INT. WINDSOR. KING'S APARTMENTS. DRAWING-ROOM. DAY

QUEEN: Two hours late. He does this on purpose. He knows it is his lateness that always drives you mad.

*She claps her hand over her mouth at this* faux pas, *but the* KING *is unperturbed.*

KING: Fear not. I shall strike a note of reconciliation. Love, that is the keynote.

FITZROY: Their Royal Highnesses, Your Majesty.

KING: (*To* DUKE OF YORK) Fred.

DUKE OF YORK: Pa.

KING: George.

DUKE OF YORK: Ma.

KING: (*Motioning them to sit*) Oh, do please.

PRINCE OF WALES: How is Your Majesty?

KING: A fat lot you care.

QUEEN: Love, George.

KING: You smile, sir.

PRINCE OF WALES: I am happy to see my father his old self and in such good spirits, sir.

KING: (*With growing anger*) Good or bad I am in control of them, sir. When a man can control himself, his spirits are

69

immaterial. When a man cannot control himself he would do
well to be sober, he would do well . . .
WILLIS *moves in as the* KING *stutters to a halt. He coughs. The*
KING *gives* WILLIS *an irritated look but recovers himself and*
*calms down.*
Marry, sir.
PRINCE OF WALES: (*With a big effort*) I am married, sir.
WILLIS *looks alarmed.*
KING: Somebody big, somebody German. Children. What, what?
PRINCE OF WALES: I am married, sir.
KING: (*Furious*) Not without my say-so. And I do not say so. I
will not say so. You are not married, sir.
WILLIS *gives a little cough. This irritates the* KING *but he visibly*
*controls himself.*
If you have a cough, sir, take it outside.
WILLIS *hesitates, then goes.*
*To* PRINCE OF WALES:
Put her away, sir. Your debts will be paid . . . and you will
have an income that is . . . appropriate.


INT. WINDSOR. LIBRARY. DAY
*The* KING *is with* PITT, *the* KING *signing warrants and state papers.*
PITT *hands him a warrant.* WILLIS *is sitting in the background,*
*waiting.*
KING: (*Looking at the warrant*) Is it any wonder a man goes mad?
Doctors. Thirty guineas a visit? And travelling expenses. For
six months' torture. They would have a man pay for his own
execution, what, what? How much is he getting?
*He looks at* WILLIS.
PITT: An annuity. £1,000 a year, sir.
KING: Well, he has done me some service.
PITT: I think it is time has done you the service, sir.
KING: Yes? Mmm . . . But what of the colonies, Mr Pitt?
PITT: America is now a nation, sir.
KING: Well, we must get used to it. I have known stranger things.
I once saw a sheep with five legs.


INT. WINDSOR. KING'S APARTMENTS. BACKSTAIRS. DAY
GREVILLE, BRAUN *and* PAPANDIEK.
BRAUN: Sacked? Jesus!

PAPANDIEK: And me? I was his Majesty's devoted servant.

BRAUN: Yes.

GREVILLE: Forget what you have seen. Majesty in its small clothes. Wipe it from your memory.

PAPANDIEK: He was ill. We knew that.

GREVILLE: Yes, and now he is well. Here.

*He throws them each a purse.*

INT. WINDSOR. LIVING-QUARTERS. GREVILLE'S ROOM. DAY

FITZROY *gives* GREVILLE *a letter. He reads it.*

GREVILLE: Me too. I am no longer in service.

FITZROY *does not look surprised.*

FITZROY: You were kind to His Majesty during his illness, Greville.

GREVILLE: I did what I could, Captain Fitzroy.

FITZROY: *Colonel* Fitzroy. Did you not know that? It seems unfair, I agree. But a word of advice. To be kind does not commend you to kings. They see it, as they see any flow of feeling, as a liberty. A blind eye will serve you better. And you will travel further.

INT. WINDSOR. KING'S APARTMENTS. BACKSTAIRS. NIGHT

GREVILLE *surprises* LADY PEMBROKE, *proceeding, in her usual stately fashion, towards the Queen's bedroom.*

GREVILLE: Elizabeth.

LADY PEMBROKE: His Majesty has yet to retire, Mr Greville.

GREVILLE: I am to leave tomorrow.

LADY PEMBROKE: Yes.

GREVILLE: You knew?

LADY PEMBROKE: It's a pity. You seemed such a promising young man.

GREVILLE: Could I . . .

*She waits without softening her expression. He tries to kiss her but she draws back.*

LADY PEMBROKE: Mr Greville, please.

GREVILLE: But . . . when . . .

LADY PEMBROKE: It was what was required, Mr Greville, that was all.

71

INT. WINDSOR. KING'S APARTMENTS. DRESSING-ROOM.
NIGHT
*They move into the dressing-room as the* KING *appears, announced by three new* PAGES.
PAGES: Sharp, sharp! The King, the King!
    *The* KING *takes* LADY PEMBROKE *out of earshot of the unhappy* GREVILLE.
KING: Madam, when I was ill they tell me I said certain things.
LADY PEMBROKE: I have no memory of them, sir.
KING: It is not so much what was said as what was done. So, did we, did we . . .
LADY PEMBROKE: Your Majesty?
KING: Did we . . . did we . . . did we ever forget ourselves utterly, because if we did forget ourselves I would so like to remember, what, what?
LADY PEMBROKE: No, sir. Your Majesty's behaviour throughout was impeccable.
KING: Heh, hey?
LADY PEMBROKE: Like the kindest father as well as the most generous of sovereigns.
KING: (*Sadly*) Good, good.


INT. WINDSOR. KING'S APARTMENTS. QUEEN'S BEDROOM.
NIGHT
*The* KING *enters. The* QUEEN *is sitting, waiting for him, on the end of the bed.*
KING: Mrs King.
QUEEN: Mr King.
KING: You're a good little pudding, what, what?
QUEEN: It was said, when you were ill, that if you had led a . . . normal life . . . this might not have happened.
KING: A normal life?
QUEEN: Other women, sir.
KING: Kicked over the traces, you mean. No life is without its regrets. Yet none is without its consolations. You are a good little woman, Mrs King. And we have been happy, have we not?
QUEEN: Oh, yes, Mr King.
    *They embrace.*

72

The King and Queen with their children on the steps of St Paul's Cathedral

KING: And shall be again.
*The* KING *makes the faintest shudder; fear shows in his eyes. He cannot tell if he is still ill or not.*

EXT. ST PAUL'S. DAY
*High shot of St Paul's, with the royal coaches arriving: flunkeys, heralds, cheering crowds, etc.*
*The* KING *and* QUEEN *draw up at the foot of St Paul's steps and get out, the* KING *turning to lift down Amelia and two other royal children.*
WILLIS, *hovering, intercepts the* KING.
WILLIS: Your Majesty, I shall be in the cathedral, should the ceremony prove to be too much of a burden for you.
*He has laid his hand on the* KING's *arm. The* KING *looks at the* QUEEN, *whose eyes urge the* KING *to dismiss* WILLIS. *A moment of suspense. Then the* KING *looks at* WILLIS's *hand, and* WILLIS *removes it.*
KING: You may tell Dr Willis that the ceremony will not be such a burden as the want of ceremony has been. And do not look at me, sir. Presume not I am the thing I was. I am not the

patient, sir. Be off with you, sir. Back to your sheep and your pigs. The King is himself again.

*The* KING *turns away.* WILLIS *puts on his hat, ready to leave. He does not look altogether unhappy.*

*The* ROYAL FAMILY *at the foot of the steps.*

*They acknowledge the crowds, among whom, standing forlornly with the common herd, we see* MARIA FITZHERBERT. *The* PRINCE OF WALES, *with an effort, ignores her.*

*The* KING *leads his family up the steps, all the time waving to the crowds.*

We must try to be more a family. There are model farms now, model villages, even model factories. Well, we must be a model family for the nation to look to.

QUEEN: (*To* DUKE OF YORK) Yes. You must try to be more typical, Fred.

PRINCE OF WALES: But Pa, I want something to *do.*

KING: Do? Well, follow in my footsteps, that is what you should do. Smile at the people. Wave to them. Let them see we are happy! That is why we are here.

*As a Handel anthem swells inside the cathedral, the* ROYAL FAMILY *wave to the crowd.* WILLIS *is at the edge of the cheering crowd and even he takes his hat off to give a modest cheer before pushing his way back through the throng and past* MARIA FITZHERBERT, *who is trying hard to smile.*

*At the top of the steps the* ROYAL FAMILY *smile and wave. Who could think they are not happy?*

*Alone in the shot* GEORGE III *takes off his hat and waves it to his people. His people wave back.*

*Before the credits there is a final caption:*

THE COLOUR OF THE KING'S URINE SUGGESTS HE WAS SUFFERING FROM PORPHYRIA, A PHYSICAL ILLNESS THAT AFFECTS THE NERVOUS SYSTEM. THE DISEASE IS PERIODIC, UNPREDICTABLE – AND HERDITARY.